OUR GOD
IS AN
AWESOME GOD

Edited by Kelly and Dede Petre

Our God Is an Awesome God

Devotional Readings on
the Nature of God

DPI
DISCIPLESHIP
PUBLICATIONS
INTERNATIONAL

Cover design: Chris Costello
Cover photo: ©1999 PhotoDisc
Interior design: Jennifer Matienzo and Chad Crossland

ISBN: 1-57782-122-X

*To the World Sector Leaders of the
International Churches of Christ:*

*You have faithfully called
us and inspired us to know and
love God above all else.*

A Special Note

It is with much excitement and joy that we introduce to you Kelly and Dede Petre, who have served as the editors for this, the eleventh volume in the Daily Power Series. Kelly graduated with honors in 1985 from Princeton University with a degree in aerospace engineering. He was baptized into Christ while a sophomore and has been serving in full-time staff ministry positions since 1986. He served the church in Paris from 1986 to 1991. Dede has a degree in French language and literature from Boston University where she became a disciple during her senior year. She also served on the staff of the Paris church from 1989 to 1991. Kelly and Dede were married there in 1990.

After returning to Boston, Kelly was appointed an evangelist and Dede a women's ministry leader, and they were sent out to lead the planting of the Montreal church in 1992. Since returning to Boston in 1994, they have led a sector on the North Shore. Kelly is training to be a church teacher under the guidance of Gordon Ferguson. They have two children, Nicolas and Haylie.

Early on, after the Petres returned from Montreal, we recognized their gifts which would make them a great asset to this publishing ministry. They have a deep love for the Scriptures and skill in expressing spiritual truths in helpful and exciting ways. We were encouraged when they agreed to begin a special assignment with DPI while still leading the ministry that they love so much. We look forward to them being involved with our publishing efforts in more ways in the future.

Kelly and Dede outlined this book and for the most part selected all the writers. They have worked long hours to edit it and get it into a form that we believe will help disciples around the world know our great and awesome God in a deeper way.

THOMAS AND SHEILA JONES
General editors, Daily Power Series

Contents

Prologue 11
Swimming in the Deep End

INTRODUCTION
1 **Getting to Know You** 17
The Amazing Opportunity to Know God   JIM BLOUGH
2 **The God Who Is** 21
Infinite, Eternal, Unchanging   KELLY PETRE
3 **God, Unlimited** 25
God Is Spirit   KAY SUMMERS MCKEAN
4 **In All He Says and Does** 29
Creator, Sustainer, Redeemer   KELLY PETRE

GOD IN CREATION
5 **Cosmic Power** 35
Our Almighty God   ANDREW GIAMBARBA
6 **The Sage of the Ages** 39
The Wisdom of God   GLORIA BAIRD
7 **Engineering 101** 43
God as Designer   GRAHAM GUMLEY, M.D.
8 **The Eye of the Beholder** 47
A God of Beauty   GERI LAING
9 **He Alone Is Good** 51
The Goodness of God   DEDE PETRE
10 **A Generous Heart** 55
The Kindness of God   MARK TEMPLER

GOD IN PROVIDENCE
11 **The Just Judge** 61
The Justice of God   NICK YOUNG
12 **Absolutely!** 65
The God of Truth   FRANÇOIS AND PENNY FAURE
13 **Straight A's** 69
An All-Knowing God   NADINE TEMPLER
14 **High and Holy** 73
The Holiness of God   ONYECHI OGUAGHA
15 **Nobody Does It Better** 77
The Perfection of God   KAREN LOUIS
16 **It's Under Control** 81
The Sovereignty of God   RON DRABOT

GOD IN REDEMPTION

17 **He Stoops Down** 87
    The Condescension of God   STEVE ROSENBAUM

18 **The Gift Giver** 91
    The Grace and Mercy of God   TAMMY FLEMING

19 **I'll Be Waiting** 95
    The Patience of God   SUNNY CHAN

20 **In Harm's Way** 99
    Our Refuge and Protector   LIN BEATY

21 **Unfailing Love** 103
    God Is Love   JOHN REUS

THREE IN ONE

22 **There Can Be Only One** 109
    The Uniqueness of God   ANNE-BRIGITTE TALIAFERRO

23 **We Three** 114
    The Trinity   DOUGLAS JACOBY

24 **Abba, Father** 118
    God, the Father   JANET FLEURANT

25 **Exact Representation** 122
    God, the Son   DENNIS YOUNG

26 **Third Person** 126
    God, the Holy Spirit   BRIAN FELUSHKO

GOD IS HERE

27 **Always Here** 133
    Aware of God   RUSS EWELL

28 **Stand Amazed** 137
    In Awe of God   DAVE EASTMAN

29 **Easy Access** 141
    Near to God   SAM POWELL

30 **Just Like Him** 145
    Imitating God   BARBARA PORTER

31 **Heart's Delight** 149
    Enjoying God   THOMAS JONES

    Epilogue 153

Prologue
Swimming in the Deep End

Our God is an awesome God:
    He reigns from heaven above
    With wisdom, power and love.
    Our God is an awesome God![*]

It had been two years since the family had vacationed at this resort, and they walked eagerly into the pool area to find a place to enjoy some fun in the sun. With a shriek of glee, the five-year-old son broke loose from his mother's hand and bounded into the "kiddie pool" with a splash. His delight turned quickly to puzzlement and then to pain as his knees and hands scraped along the floor of the shallow pool. *What happened?* he wondered, as his mom retrieved him from the swimming pool and attended to his minor abrasions.

Kneeling down to verify that he was all right, the lifeguard gently informed the boy, "You're too big to play in this pool any more. It's time for you to join your parents and the older kids in the big pool."

✧

For many Christians, this story parallels a pressing need in our walk with God. We jumped in and came to know enough about God to satisfy our spiritual needs as young disciples. But to grow to maturity, to become men and women capable of defining Christianity for this generation, a shallow understanding of God will not suffice.

This book is designed to challenge and expand our understanding of who God is so that we may have a more meaningful relationship with him. It is intended to direct us into deep waters, waters that remain untouched for far too many in our churches today. It is an appeal to consider the unbounded nature and attributes of our infinite God. It is a call to venture into the deep end of the pool, where challenging concepts and greater satisfaction await every child of God.

*Mullins, Rich. Copyright 1988 Edward Grant, Inc. Adm. by BMG songs, Inc. ASCAP.

✧

A brother in Christ once told me that "it would do most Christians a world of good to study at least a little theology." I have had conversations with many more disciples, however, in which the mere mention of the word "theology" has elicited a reaction nearer to disdain! Many seem to associate the coldness, lack of impact or even irrelevance of their former religious experience with the idea of theology. In the opinion of some, theology serves only to remove church leaders and seminarians from the realities of modern life and meaningful faith. There may be an element of truth to these sentiments, yet we must always be careful not to let the pendulum swing too far when reacting to powerless religion.

"Theology," put simply, is the study of the nature, person and work of God, from two Greek words: *theos* which means "God" and *logos* which means "word, speech, teaching, reason." It is a rational inquiry into questions of God and his dealings with our universe. Surely no Christian could object to that! There are most certainly improper theological methods leading to theological errors great and small. Nevertheless, it would seem to me that the more prevalent source of deadness in "Christian" religion lies not so much in wrong knowledge about God as in the lack of applying that knowledge to everyday life.

The importance of theology to the church today has been downplayed in many ways. An axiom commonly preached among us goes something like this: "You can know a lot *about* someone without really *knowing* the person." (I could not agree more, because I am one of the common preachers who commonly says so!) Having a head full of notions about God does not constitute a personal relationship with him. Yet understand this: You cannot really know a person *without* knowing a lot about them. Our goal here is not to promote knowledge of God as an end in itself. Instead, it remains a hallmark of our movement to emphasize a relationship with God as the goal and outcome of true Christianity. Prayerfully, knowing better who God is will only help to deepen our relationship with him.

✧

We are excited to once again have contributors to this volume from ministries around the world. Men and women from every world sector of the International Churches of Christ have wrestled with the Scriptures and their own experiences in order to spur us along in our journey of understanding the awesome God we serve. Decide from the outset to deepen your own knowledge of him as you consider the questions at the end of each chapter and dig into the Bible for yourself. Use these daily devotionals as a jumping-off point into the deep end of your own study of God.

And this is my prayer: that your love may abound more and more in knowledge and depth of insight, so that you may be able to discern what is best and may be pure and blameless until the day of Christ, filled with the fruit of righteousness that comes through Jesus Christ—to the glory and praise of God. (Philippians 1:9-11)

May our awesome God bless your efforts as you strive to know him more and more. And now—let's jump in!

KELLY PETRE
Boston, USA
July 1999

INTRODUCTION

1

Getting to Know You
The Amazing Opportunity to Know God

JIM BLOUGH
Washington D.C., USA

"To know God." A simple phrase, yet one that describes life's most amazing opportunity! Is it really possible for man, mere man, to actually *know God?* Solomon, the wisest man of the Old Testament period, contemplated the temple he had built and meditated:

> "But will God really dwell on earth with men? The heavens, even the highest heavens, cannot contain you. How much less this temple I have built!" (2 Chronicles 6:18)

Moses, when confronted with the challenge of leading God's people, realized his desperate need to know God: "If you are pleased with me, teach me your ways so I may know you and continue to find favor with you" (Exodus 33:13). Jesus, God's only Son, realized the incredible, life-transforming power of knowing God when he prayed, "Now this is eternal life: that they may know you, the only true God, and Jesus Christ, whom you have sent" (John 17:3).

We desperately need to know God, but the challenge seems over-whelming because God is so different from us: all-powerful, absolutely pure, infinitely merciful, completely righteous. We have all had the experience of trying to get to know someone from a very different background—it seems we have nothing in common, no middle ground, nothing to build on. It takes one of us—usually the bolder or more mature one—to take the initiative and reach out to make the relation-ship possible. Incredibly, this is exactly what God has done with us. We *can* know God because he wants us to know him. God has so completely revealed himself to us that we can know him, intimately, as a best friend!

It is God's humility, his openness and his willingness to expose his heart to us that makes knowing him possible.

General Mail

How has God revealed himself to us? First, through "general revelation" he has disclosed himself to all people, at all times and in all places. Consider this passage:

> The heavens declare the glory of God;
>   the skies proclaim the work of his hands.
> Day after day they pour forth speech;
>   night after night they display knowledge.
> There is no speech or language
>   where their voice is not heard.
> Their voice goes out into all the earth,
>   their words to the ends of the world. (Psalm 19:1-4)

God has revealed so much of himself through nature. His creativity is obvious in the thousands of different species of animals and plants that populate our planet. His power and bounty are evident in the millions of stars that fill the night sky. His care and concern can be seen from the way he sends rain in season to water the earth (see Acts 14:17). Even the incredible creation that God has made testifies to this very existence.

> For since the creation of the world God's invisible qualities—his eternal power and divine nature—have been clearly seen, being understood from what has been made, so that men are without excuse. (Romans 1:20)

God also reveals himself through the spirit he has put inside every man: "So God created man in his own image, in the image of God he created him; male and female he created them" (Genesis 1:27). What does it mean that God has created man in his image? Surely it is that we can think and feel, can know and be known, can love and be loved, and can understand right and wrong. Every man has both a God-given sense of eternity and a gnawing awareness of death deep in his soul (see Ecclesiastes 3:11, Hebrews 2:15, Romans 2:14-15). This inner knowledge of God written on our hearts is part of God's revelation to us as well.

I often thought about God as I took science courses and pondered the world around me. I was especially aware of God when I knew I had sinned and my conscience convicted me! But the knowledge of God that comes from looking at nature and listening to our hearts can go only so far. I did not really come to know God until the point in time when I was confronted by his Word and he entered my life in a personal way.

Special Delivery

The good news is that God has not simply left vague traces of himself for us to decipher. He has further disclosed himself to specific people at specific times in specific places. The record of this "special revelation" is what we call the Bible!

Special revelation is personal: God comes and reveals not just himself, but a particular plan for our lives. What must Abram have felt when he heard the words:

> "Leave your country, your people and your father's household and go to the land I will show you.
>
> > I will make you into a great nation
> > > and I will bless you;
> > I will make your name great,
> > > and you will be a blessing.
> > I will bless those who bless you,
> > > and whoever curses you I will curse;
> > and all peoples on earth
> > > will be blessed through you." (Genesis 12:1-3)

God's individual plan for our lives reveals still more of his heart and his desire to bless us and care for us. I will never forget the night in November of 1977 when Ryan Howard taught me from the Scriptures that God wanted to know me and that he had a specific plan for my life. Ryan was the first of many men God would use to shape my life through more than twenty years in his kingdom. His special revelation is found in his word, but it is often given special delivery treatment by other men and women. Wanting us to know him and his plan, God puts the right people in our lives, and we need to be humbly grateful for that.

Special revelation is personal and exciting, but we must be ready for it to be painful as well. Paul teaches us that the only way to fully know Christ is to share in his sufferings:

I want to know Christ and the power of his resurrection and the fellowship of sharing in his sufferings, becoming like him in his death, and so, somehow, to attain to the resurrection from the dead. (Philippians 3:10-11)

More than anything else, what has helped me to know God and to seek and feel his presence in my life has been suffering. When we suffer, we understand more about what was in God's heart as he watched his only Son die on the cross for our sins and as he reaches out to a lost world. I dare say that if you are afraid to suffer, you will never really know God.

God has truly gone the extra mile to give us the opportunity to know him. Generally, through his creation, and in a special way, through Jesus and the inspired Word, he opens wide his heart to all who would make the effort to seek him. Respond to his revelation. Turn your heart to him. Get to know your God!

God and You

1. What motivates you to want to know God?

2. What have you learned about God through observing his creation? Describe something you would not know about God were it not for your study of the Bible.

3. Who are the men and women who have helped you to know God through the Scriptures and through their lives? What have you learned about God from them that you are most grateful to have learned?

4. What about knowing God is most amazing to you?

2

The God Who Is
Infinite, Eternal, Unchanging

KELLY PETRE
Boston, USA

A book on the nature of God cannot help but wade into concepts that are difficult for our limited minds to grasp. Like a blind person striving to understand "color" or a deaf person endeavoring to comprehend a symphony, our physical limitations inhibit us from fully fathoming the nature of our God. In many ways, he is everything we are not. But if we are going to appreciate our relationship with him and marvel at the grace that brings it about, we must do the hard work of contemplating his greatness.

The Bible reveals that God exists independently of his creation. "In the beginning, God…" (Genesis 1:1). When revealing himself to Moses,

> God said to Moses, "I AM WHO I AM. This is what you are to say to the Israelites: "I AM has sent me to you." (Exodus 3:14)

God exists. He is. And he is who he is. He exists outside of time and space, for time and space are dimensions of our material universe that he created. He alone has life independently of any environment where he chooses to make himself known. "For as the Father has life in himself, so he has granted the Son to have life in himself" (John 5:26).

As we set out to better know our God, we will consider three aspects of his nature that proceed from the fact of his self-existence: God is infinite, he is eternal, and he is forever unchanging.

Omni

When speaking of God as infinite, we pass entirely out of the realm of personal experience. "If only I had been there in time" is an oft-heard lament in dramatic films. But "here" and "there" are all the same to God, and time is of no consequence to the Almighty One.

Where can I go from your Spirit?
> Where can I flee from your presence?
If I go up to the heavens, you are there;
> if I make my bed in the depths, you are there.
If I rise on the wings of the dawn,
> if I settle on the far side of the sea,
even there your hand will guide me,
> your right hand will hold me fast. (Psalm 139:7-10)

God is completely unlimited. Theologians have attached the Latin prefix *omni*—meaning "all"—to numerous words in order to invent a vocabulary that can only be used when describing the infinite nature of God. With regard to space, he is omnipresent. As for his power and understanding, God is omnipotent and omniscient. Big words—big God!

In practical terms, his infinity leads us to understand two important characteristics of the God who is. First, God is *transcendent*. This means—in opposition to many Eastern religious views, New Age philosophies and nature religions—that God is distinct from and infinitely exalted above the creation. Nature cannot "contain" him, any more than an artist is "contained in" or "the same as" his painting. He is the sovereign Creator and Judge of the universe.

Second, God is *immanent*. His presence and power pervade everything, from the tiniest molecule to the innermost thoughts of men's hearts. Although not confined in his creation, God is not the far-removed, impersonal force of the Deists.

For this is what the high and lofty One says—
> he who lives forever, whose name is holy:
"I live in a high and holy place,
> but also with him who is contrite and lowly in spirit,
to revive the spirit of the lowly
> and to revive the heart of the contrite." (Isaiah 57:15)

"The God who made the world and everything in it is the Lord of heaven and earth and does not live in temples built by hands. And he is not served by human hands, as if he needed anything, because he himself gives all men life and breath and everything else...though he is not far from each one of us. 'For in him we live and move and have our being.'" (Acts 17:24-25, 27b-28)

How wonderful, how incomprehensible are the ways of our limit-less God! How offensive to limit him to the dimensions of idols made by our hands or our minds!

All the Time

Before the mountains were born
  or you brought forth the earth and the world,
    from everlasting to everlasting you are God. (Psalm 90:2)

"I am the Alpha and the Omega," says the Lord God, "who is, and who was, and who is to come, the Almighty." (Revelation 1:8)

The Scriptures clearly teach that God transcends time as well as space. While God is sensitive to the passage of time, he is not bound by it, and he is able to act in history as he sees fit.

But do not forget this one thing, dear friends: With the Lord a day is like a thousand years, and a thousand years are like a day. (2 Peter 3:8)

Consider the staggering implications of this fact when it comes to our prayers—we may be bound by time, but God is not! He sees the past, present and future as a continuous *now*, a perpetual "Today" (Psalm 2:7, 2 Corinthians 6:2, Hebrews 4:7). He is able to carry out his designs for tomorrow as we fervently pray to him today!

Still the Same

Finally, knowing that God is the great I AM teaches us that he is *immutable*, that he does not change.

[The earth and the heavens] will perish, but you [God] remain;
  they will all wear out like a garment.
Like clothing you will change them
  and they will be discarded.
But you remain the same,
  and your years will never end. (Psalm 102:26-27)

The great deeds enacted by God in times past were accomplished by the same God we serve today. He cannot grow older, wiser, stronger, weaker or in any way different than who he has always been. The truth of his word (Isaiah 40:6-8, Psalm 119:89, 151-52), the glories of his character (Exodus 34:5-7, Hebrews 13:8, James 1:17) and the purposes of his heart (1 Samuel 15:29, Numbers 23:19, Psalm 33:11) remain constant throughout eternity. The handful of passages in the Revised Standard Version and the King James Version of the Bible which speak of God as "repenting" (Genesis 6:6-7, 1 Samuel 15:11, 2 Samuel 24:16, Jonah 3:10, Joel 2:13-14) simply attest to his consistency in dealing with people according to his nature when *they* had changed. There is no insinuation that their actions were unforeseen, and no changes made to the eternal purpose and plan of God. Very simply, we can "know and rely on the love God has for us" (1 John 4:16).

We live in a world where we are bound by physical limitations. Let us dare to draw near to the limitless God who made us, in anticipation of the sure hope that he will one day bring us into his glorious presence.

God and You

1. *In what ways has your view of God placed limitations on how you believe he can act in your life?*

2. *How will understanding that God is bigger than history affect the way you pray?*

3. *Do you feel secure in your relationship with God? How does he want you to feel, given the unchanging nature of his faithfulness?*

4. *Seeing God as he is always leads to humility. Spend some time in awesome praise of the God who is.*

3
God, Unlimited
God Is Spirit

KAY SUMMERS MCKEAN
Boston, USA

"Sir," the woman said, "I can see that you are a prophet. Our fathers worshiped on this mountain, but you Jews claim that the place where we must worship is in Jerusalem."

Jesus declared, "Believe me, woman, a time is coming when you will worship the Father neither on this mountain nor in Jerusalem. You Samaritans worship what you do not know; we worship what we do know, for salvation is from the Jews. Yet a time is coming and has now come when the true worshipers will worship the Father in spirit and truth, for they are the kind of worshipers the Father seeks. God is spirit, and his worshipers must worship in spirit and in truth."

John 4:19-24

Reading the conversations Jesus had with people about religion is fascinating. This particular episode involves a rather outspoken woman who thought she had a lot of things figured out. But she hadn't figured out God! Certainly, her understanding was accurate regarding the Jews' devotion to worship in Jerusalem. The Israelites had indeed been given the Holy City as the center of their religious life. The Samaritans, on the other hand, argued that Mt. Gerazim was the place to find God. At this point in the Samaritan woman's life, her confusion was based on "Where?"; Jesus instead directed her mind to "Who?"

No Bounds

Centuries earlier, when the temple in Jerusalem was brand new, King Solomon observed:

"But will God really dwell on earth with men? The heavens, even the highest heavens, cannot contain you. How much less this temple I have built!" (2 Chronicles 6:18)

As much as the Jews revered their holy place, there was an understanding that God was greater than a place on the map. Jesus' declaration that "God is spirit" may have confused this Samaritan woman even more, because her next remark shows that she wanted clarification: "I know that Messiah is coming. When he comes, he will explain everything to us" (John 4:25).

"God is spirit" *is* a bit hard to understand, isn't it? As a child, I had many pictures in my mind of God: An old man with a beard and flowing robes, or perhaps something as aesthetic as the massive God of Michelangelo's masterpiece reaching out his hand to create Adam. I learned with time, of course, that there were no "pictures" of God, which left me with a vague uneasiness. If he could not be seen, did he really exist? In fact there was nothing that my physical senses could perceive about God. I could not see him, smell him, touch him, taste him or hear him.

This very troubling aspect of God has caused many through the centuries to explain God through graven images, religious creeds, symbols, ceremonies and traditions. God has been dissected, analyzed, studied and theorized. Why? Because our human nature cannot stand it when we do not know *exactly* what we are dealing with. We yearn to be in control, and we cannot control what does not easily fit into a jar like a specimen.

The truth is, God will not allow us to treat him like a specimen. God *is* spirit, which means he will not be bound by physical limitations. Those limitations are restricting, and God cannot be restricted. He created physical space, he created time, he created all of the dimensions, but he will not be bound by them.

I recently read a story about a little boy, sitting at his kitchen table, drawing with his crayons. He seemed to be quite intense about his project, so his mother asked him, "What are you drawing?"

"God," the little boy answered.

The mother was surprised and said gently, "But son, no one knows what God looks like!"

The boy looked at his mother and said with confidence, "That's why I have to finish this picture—so that people will know!"

This story demonstrates our tendency to want to comprehend God in our own ways, usually so that God can fit into the mold of what we want. We are tempted to think that if God can be explained and comprehended, then he can be manipulated. We can then make God into our own image and bid him to do our will.

The good news is that because God is spirit, he is far greater than our own imaginings. He is not cramped by human limitations; therefore he can do more (Ephesians 3:21). God can deal with more than one of us at a time, in more than one place at a time, and he can do that all the time. The fact that we cannot comprehend him perfectly does not mean that he will do less in our lives; in fact it means he can do more! It means that I do not have to go to a certain place for God to hear my prayers; he can hear me from wherever I may be. It means he can hear disciples praying around the world all at the same time and not grow weary. It means that even if I don't say the "perfect" thing to my friend about Jesus, God can work in her heart, anyway. It means that God can see my heart as well as my actions.

Spirits in a Material World

God is spirit, and "God created man in his own image" (Genesis 1:27). What does this tell me? It tells me that the most important part of every human being on the face of this earth is the spiritual part of them. God did create us with a spirit, with that intangible part of us that wants to know him. It is imperative that I view myself in this way: a spiritual person with a longing to know God. I am very grateful that God has revealed this to me, and I live my life striving that my spirit will be one with his. This is also how I must view others. Each person I meet has a spiritual side to him or her, and that spiritual side desires intimacy with the Creator. Too many have drowned out their spiritual natures with materialism and doubt and sin. It is my lifelong task to reconnect others with God, so that their spirits can be refreshed and whole again.

It is a joy to learn more and more about God. This very book is aimed at teaching us all about his attributes, his nature and his greatness. Yet the more I learn, the more I realize there is to learn! God is immeasurable. We will never figure him out completely, nor should we presume to do so. Because God is spirit, he is bigger, deeper, higher and greater than all we can imagine. As we grow closer to him, our spirits will soar to greater heights than we ever dreamed possible.

God and You

1. *How did the Samaritan woman's limited view of God affect her life? How has your view of God been limiting?*

2. *Why is the commandment in Exodus 20:4 ("You shall not make for yourself an idol...") so important for our understanding that "God is spirit"?*

3. *In what ways have you tried to make God more tangible and controllable?*

4. *Our finite minds cannot completely understand the infinite qualities of God. How do you feel about trusting in a being whom you cannot totally comprehend?*

4

In All He Says and Does
Creator, Sustainer, Redeemer

KELLY PETRE
Boston, USA

Shallow. Have you ever felt that way about your own understanding of who God really is? I have caught myself at various points in my Christian life praying with so limited a vocabulary that you would think God could be contained in a Cracker Jack box. And yet, the God of the Bible is so vast that we complex humans are compared to grasshoppers in the face of his greatness (Isaiah 40:22). How important it is that we go beyond our limited view of God and strive to know him as he truly is! How enriching and fulfilling to discover new facets of the divine character!

When we finally do delve into a study of God's character and attributes, we are immediately humbled by how many amazing qualities he displays, each one meriting our attention and devotion. Attempting to understand all these attributes of God can be like trying to take a sip from a fire hose. Is it really possible to understand the character of an infinite, eternal, invisible God? Even with the aid of God's self-revelation, his word, it still becomes necessary to develop some sort of framework to make sense of it all.

My Father

One of the greatest undeserved blessings of my life is to have been raised in a family who truly loved me. My mom and dad were, and still are, incredible examples of what caring parents ought to be.

I am fortunate to know my father well. Just what do I mean by this? As a boy, I caught glimpses of his heart in the encouragement—and discipline—that I received. I hold on to countless lessons learned in laughter and in tears. And while I felt close to my dad even then, it is clear that I know him much better today, having now seen him in roles other than simply as "my dad."

The day came when I learned more about his own childhood, and through this understanding, I came to admire him all the more for his cheerful, easygoing nature, his capacity to overcome, and his courage to chart a new course for his own life. As a boy, I understood little of his business dealings; but the more I have learned about his accomplishments as a real estate developer and entrepreneur, the more I marvel at his integrity and hard-work ethic, his optimism and the respect he has won among his peers.

Over time I stopped taking for granted the number of lifelong friendships he and my mom had developed and maintain to this day. And since getting married myself, I have been more appreciative of the way he is as a husband. Again and again I have been convicted by his attentiveness to my mom's needs and his cheerful and serving spirit around the house. I could go on, but my point is simply that observing my father as dad, husband, businessman, son and friend has allowed me to see more clearly the heart of the man who is my father. Certain qualities and attributes are more readily apparent as I consider him in these various roles.

Our Father

The same is true of God. Appreciating God is like appreciating a fine diamond. We can easily say, "Wow, isn't that pretty! Look at it sparkle!" In reality, however, a lot is happening all at once to cause us to marvel at the beauty of the gem. Its brilliance can be attributed to the complex action of light as it is reflected and refracted across many, many facets. This is a fitting parallel for the daunting task of striving to "know" our infinite God.

God cannot be squeezed into a box. We can easily sing, "Our God is an awesome God!" Yet his character is more beautiful, his glory more brilliant than the finest of diamonds. He is many amazing things all at once. Can we ever hope to know him?

I believe that by considering certain facets of his character individually, we really can get to know him more deeply. Furthermore, the individual qualities of God's greatness stand out more starkly as we consider him acting in his various roles. As with my earthly father, I can come to know the heart of God as I contemplate these divine roles.

First of all, God is the Creator of everything that is.

In the beginning God created the heavens and the earth.
(Genesis 1:1)

Do you not know?
    Have you not heard?
The Lord is the everlasting God,
    the Creator of the ends of the earth.
He will not grow tired or weary,
    and his understanding no one can fathom.
(Isaiah 40:28)

Looking closely at the chapters in the next part of this book on God in creation, you will find that his power, wisdom and goodness are displayed in an amazing way.

Second, God is the Great Sustainer, meaning he doesn't create the world and leave it as an orphan while he goes on to contemplate his own greatness. No, he remains involved. His providence in the affairs of the universe is very real.

"I am he who will sustain you.
I have made you and I will carry you;
    I will sustain you and I will rescue you." (Isaiah 46:4)

For the Lord is our judge,
    the Lord is our lawgiver,
the Lord is our king;
    it is he who will save us. (Isaiah 33:22)

"Are not two sparrows sold for a penny? Yet not one of them will fall to the ground apart from the will of your Father."
(Matthew 10:29)

"You gave me life and showed me kindness,
    and in your providence watched over my spirit." (Job 10:12)

As we look at God in providence, we will see his justice, truth and holiness.

Third, we can view God in his role as Redeemer.

"With everlasting kindness
    I will have compassion on you,"
        says the Lord your Redeemer. (Isaiah 54:8)

"Then you will know that I, the LORD, am your Savior,
      your Redeemer, the Mighty One of Jacob." (Isaiah 60:16b)

God our Savior...wants all men to be saved and to come to a
knowledge of the truth. (1 Timothy 2:3-4)

As we look at God in redemption, we will see clearly his mercy, his condescension, his great love.

In each and every one of the attributes I've mentioned, God is infinite, eternal and unchanging. Let that one sink in. What an amazing God we serve! What an incredible heart! How rich and unfathomable are the depths of his greatness! And while each of these excellent qualities overlap in his roles of Creator, Sustainer and Redeemer, these stand out the most: As Creator, his wisdom, knowledge, power and goodness; as Sustainer, his justice, truth and holiness; as Redeemer, his mercy, condescension and love.

Viewing God's character through these facets of his activity will serve as a framework for the rest of the book. There is no perfect way to proceed, but hopefully this will provide a jumping-off point for your own contemplation of God's immeasurable glory.

God and You

1. *How deep is your knowledge of God? Using your prayer life as a barometer, for what kinds of things do you praise God?*

2. *Consider any one of God's qualities, for example, his mercy. What does it mean that his mercy is infinite? Eternal? Unchanging? Do the same for his justice...his wisdom...his holiness...his love.*

3. *Is your relationship with God truly a relationship? Are you striving to know the personality and character of God more and more? Are you drawing nearer to the God who is?*

4. *Begin to catalogue God's amazing attributes yourself. Stand in awe as you see the list grow over the coming weeks.*

GOD IN
CREATION

5

Cosmic Power
Our Almighty God

ANDREW GIAMBARBA
Miami, USA

When God created this world, he spoke order out of chaos. When he created the mountains, he spoke their height and their breadth. He created their slopes and their peaks. He created their impenetrable faces and set one next to another in miles of ranges. I remember crossing the Andes Mountains in a bus with the mission team from Buenos Aires as we went to plant the church in Santiago, Chile. I remember feeling absolutely insignificant as I looked up at their grandeur. And then it hit me: What if God were the size of these mountains? Would I have any problem trusting him with the future of this mission team if he were as big as the Andes? Would not I walk through the streets of Santiago like the man with the most support in the world if my God were the size of the mountains? And yet the Scriptures teach:

> The mountains melt like wax before the Lord,
>   before the Lord of all the earth. (Psalm 97:5)

> Before the mountains were born
>   or you brought forth the earth and the world,
>   from everlasting to everlasting you are God. (Psalm 90:2)

I love the ocean. Living in Miami, I have the opportunity to take my son out fishing whenever I can rope someone into it who has a boat. Last summer he and I were sixteen miles offshore in the middle of a fishing trip when the swells started to reach eight to ten feet. My son started to get scared as we turned to head in. I had him sit on my lap, and I wrapped my arms around him. As we rolled around on the way home, I had such a great time telling him that just as I had him tight in my arms and would never let him go, so God had both of us wrapped tight in his. My "power" was enough to calm the fears of my son and to make him think about the fish that we had caught instead of worrying about "what if...." And yet the Scriptures teach:

> "Who shut up the sea behind doors
>   when it burst forth from the womb,
> when I made the clouds its garment
>   and wrapped it in thick darkness,
> when I fixed limits for it
>   and set its doors and bars in place,
> when I said, 'This far you may come and no farther;
>   here is where your proud waves halt'?" (Job 38:8-11)

Power That Protects

I am writing this article from the mission field in Lima, Peru. My wife and I have brought our two children to a place that the State Department of the US calls "extremely dangerous," although the terrorist attacks are more "sporadic" since 1995. My wife was converted on the mission field in Buenos Aires. We went through death threats, typhoid fever, miscarriages, "and the like" in our first years of marriage.

But then we moved back to the Unites States in 1993 and our kids started to grow up. We began thinking much more about meeting the neighbors and the teachers than wondering about death threats. When the Central and South America World Sector sent out the last mission team to fulfill our responsibility to plant a church in every nation with a city of 100,000 or more people, Mari and I jumped at the chance to spend our summer in Latin America leading the planting. Yet as the send-off approached, I started worrying about the safety of my little daughter. In our first night here, Mari and she were crossing the road and fell flat in the middle of the street as the oncoming traffic barreled down on them. Is God powerful enough to keep them safe? The Scriptures say:

> When they were but few in number,
>   few indeed, and strangers in it,
> they wandered from nation to nation,
>   from one kingdom to another.
> He allowed no one to oppress them;
>   for their sake he rebuked kings:
> "Do not touch my anointed ones;
>   do my prophets no harm." (Psalm 105:12-15)

God is the only one with power in this universe. We hear the thunder and feel the power in a bolt of lightning, and say "God is so powerful!" We say this because it is the limit of "powerful" in our mentality. Hurricanes, tornadoes, tsunamis—they are magnificent and terrifying examples of the force of wind and rain and the ocean. But the power of God? The displays of nature in our world speak eloquently about the power of God, and yet they are only a small indication of how much he really has.

Power That Destroys Fear

The word "omnipotent" (all-powerful) can only be used when describing God. So, what does this mean for me? Everything. I believe the biggest stumbling block in this world is fear. Although God encourages us frequently in his word—"Do not be afraid"—thousands of Christians are still handcuffed by fears that an understanding of our all-powerful God should have helped us to overcome. According to the Scriptures, God created this magnificent world for us to dwell in for clearly defined reasons: to give us insight into his power and to take away our excuses (Romans 1:20).

There are not enough pages in this book to speak eloquently about the amazing power displayed by the solar system. Words could never do justice to the power and intricacy of the electrical impulses that our nervous systems send out with such amazing exactness. We could write one chapter on "bioluminescence" alone—the way God created animals who live thousands of meters under the sea to give off "cold" light with no electrical charge.

We must look to God's creation to see his power and to help us put to death our excuses born of fear. From what does our fear always keep us? Our potential to bear fruit. Fear always makes us settle for little to no impact when God wants us to be abundantly fruitful. Jesus taught:

> "I tell you the truth, unless a kernel of wheat falls to the ground and dies, it remains only a single seed. But if it dies, it produces many seeds." (John 12:24)

God wants our one life to reproduce itself many times. He is powerful enough to help us accomplish this.

God created a fern which is abundant in Florida. This single plant, typically overlooked on the floor of the swamp, contains over one billion spores—all of which could become another fern. Not even a tidal wave can compare with that kind of power!

If our all-powerful God lends a lowly fern that kind of potential power, how much more power will he "lend" to me as I strive to reproduce myself by making disciples of all nations? Let us stand in awe of God's power as we set out to make an impact on this world!

God and You

1. *What is your favorite aspect of nature? Specifically, how does it display God's power?*

2. *Write down some of your fears. First, list some of your physical fears. Next, your spiritual fears. Leave some space after each one for the next question.*

3. *After each of the fears, write out "But my God is..." and then list qualities of God that can help you overcome those fears.*

4. *Why does it make perfect sense that the God of the cosmos can use your life to produce fruit and help others to come to know him?*

6
The Sage of the Ages
The Wisdom of God

GLORIA BAIRD
Los Angeles, USA

God's wisdom—infinite! Immeasurable! Unlimited! Inconceivable! Unfathomable! Just after I wrote these words, a sister called me to get some "words of wisdom." My response was, "I am writing a chapter on God's wisdom; I've got a very humble view of my own wisdom right now!" In reality I should always have that view. God is omniscient—all-knowing. He is the source of all knowledge and wisdom.

God's Wisdom Displayed

By wisdom the Lord laid the earth's foundations,
   by understanding he set the heavens in place.
(Proverbs 3:19)

The wisdom of God is magnificently displayed in creation. God's wisdom is seen in the amazing foresight and preparation that went into making a world suitable for human beings. Before each of our three girls was born, we eagerly planned and worked to have the nursery decorated, the crib in place and baby clothes, diapers and bottles ready. How much more did God in his unlimited wisdom prepare for the birth of his children! From God's first act of creation, we see him readying the "nursery" before man was even made. His initial command, "Let there be light" (Genesis 1:3), began his preparation for us. You see, we need light; God does not, as David acknowledged in Psalm 139:12: "even the darkness will not be dark to you; the night will shine like the day, for darkness is as light to you." Furthermore, we need day and night; God does not—I marvel at God's plan to renew our strength and energy while we sleep at night. What an ingenious design! How often we take God's work for granted.

In his wisdom, God created the world in such a way that it helps us to understand who he is. For example, consider the ocean. It possesses a calming force, reminding me of the vastness of God's knowledge and the constancy of his love. Prayer walks along the beach put me back in touch with God's perspective as I surrender my burdens to him. Or think about—as Jesus urged us in Matthew 6—the birds of the air and the lilies of the field. Seeing how God takes care of these little creatures helps me to fight anxious thoughts and feelings. Al and I are currently in the midst of another move and are looking for a place to live. Certainly the Creator of the universe can meet our housing needs!

God's Wisdom Personified

The stark contrast between God's wisdom and the "wisdom" of man is clearly described in 1 Corinthians 1:22-25:

> Jews demand miraculous signs and Greeks look for wisdom, but we preach Christ crucified: a stumbling block to Jews and foolishness to Gentiles, but to those whom God has called, both Jews and Greeks, Christ the power of God and the wisdom of God. For the foolishness of God is wiser than man's wisdom, and the weakness of God is stronger than man's strength.

The world is groping for answers to life's many questions. God's emphatic answer to our questions is Jesus. The wisdom of God is personified in Christ. His life, death and resurrection respond to our deepest questions in a way no textbook or philosophy ever could. Without Jesus, our "wisdom" is nothing more than blind foolishness.

The Beginning of Wisdom

If we ever want to truly understand God's wisdom, we must go "back to the beginning":

> The fear of the Lord is the beginning of wisdom,
>   and knowledge of the Holy One is understanding.
> (Proverbs 9:10)

It is sad to see the pain and devastation caused when we ignore God's wisdom. Working to help people involved in all types of sins, I have often found myself asking, "Where is the fear of God?" More and more, I am convinced that this is a missing piece in the hearts of too many disciples. They only think of the fear of God as being afraid of God's anger and punishment. While that is a part of it, the most vital aspects are missing—reverence, awe and respect. We can't begin to know the wisdom of God until we understand what it is to fear him.

One of the defining examples of the fear of God was Job's encounter with him. After a few questions from God, Job was quickly put in his place. God challenged Job to answer his questions:

> "Where were you when I laid the earth's foundation?
>   Tell me, if you understand....
> "On what were its footings set,
>   or who laid its cornerstone?...
> "Have you ever given orders to the morning,
>   or shown the dawn its place?...
> "What is the way to the abode of light?
>   And where does darkness reside?"
> (Job 38:4, 6, 12, 19)

Totally humbled, Job finally replied to the Lord:

> "I know that you can do all things;
>   no plan of yours can be thwarted.
>
> You asked, 'Who is this that obscures my counsel without
>   knowledge?'
>   Surely I spoke of things I did not understand,
>   things too wonderful for me to know."
> "My ears had heard of you
>   but now my eyes have seen you.
> Therefore I despise myself
>   and repent in dust and ashes." (Job 42:2-3, 5-6)

Simply defined, the fear of the Lord is seeing who God is—*really*—and seeing who I am—*really*! We must see the gigantic chasm that exists between God's righteousness and our sinfulness. The fear of God brings us to humility and gratitude as we recognize that only the sacrifice of Jesus can bridge that chasm for us. The person who fears God is motivated to trust him, to live his life in obedience to him and to avoid sinning.

In his book, *The Joy of Fearing God*, Jerry Bridges gives several characteristics of a God-fearing person. He lives his life under the authority of God, acknowledging that Jesus is Lord and helping others to do the same. He is conscious of the presence of God, as well as of his dependence on God. Fearing God means living to the glory of God, desiring to honor and please him in all things above self and others.

Studying about the fear of God and striving to practice it daily has changed my life. I have reexamined my motivation—why do I share my faith? Why do I want to be fruitful? Why do I serve others? What will keep me pure and honest when no one is looking? The fear of the Lord truly is the beginning of wisdom.

The wise man Solomon, after examining his life and the lessons he learned, said:

> Now all has been heard;
>   here is the conclusion of the matter:
> Fear God and keep his commandments,
>   for this is the whole duty of man. (Ecclesiastes 12:13)

As we embrace the God of all wisdom, and Jesus Christ, who is the wisdom of God, we become part of God's master plan for our lives. Now that is good news worth sharing!

God and You

1. *What is your real attitude toward God's wisdom as compared to your wisdom? How is this demonstrated in your speech and actions?*

2. *Is your perspective of God's wisdom in creation different from your perspective of God's wisdom in your daily life? If so, how?*

3. *In what ways do you see the wisdom of God displayed in Jesus' life, death and resurrection? What questions of yours did God answer by sending Jesus?*

4. *What does the fear of God mean to you? Why is this an important motivation for you in living your life for God?*

7

Engineering 101
God as Designer

GRAHAM GUMLEY, M.D.
Phnom Penh, Cambodia

"But ask the animals, and they will teach you,
    or the birds of the air, and they will tell you;
or speak to the earth, and it will teach you,
    or let the fish of the sea inform you.
Which of all these does not know
    that the hand of the Lord has done this?
In his hand is the life of every creature
    and the breath of all mankind."

Job 12:7-11

The more I learn about the design of the universe, from the grandeur of the galaxies to the beauty of human anatomy, from the complexity of DNA to the precision of atomic particles, the more I am in awe of the power of God and the beauty of his design—and the more humble I feel at his personal involvement in my life. David realized this long before particle accelerators were invented:

When I consider your heavens,
    the work of your fingers,
the moon and the stars,
    which you have set in place,
what is man that you are mindful of him,
    the son of man that you care for him?
You made him a little lower than the heavenly beings
    and crowned him with glory and honor. (Psalm 8:3-5)

Scientists recognize that for there to be any form of life on earth, there must have been, and there must still be, incredibly detailed fine-tuning of the myriad of variables that impose themselves on our fragile existence. Current scientific thinking is that "at a particular instant roughly twelve billion years ago, all the matter and energy that we can observe [was] concentrated in a region smaller than a dime."[1] This is a staggering amount of energy, and yet it is believed that if the energy at this "Big Bang" was different by one part in ten with 120 zeros after it, there would be no life anywhere in the universe.[2] According to the widely quoted astrophysicist Michael Turner from the University of Chicago, the likelihood of this fine-tuning occurring by chance is as "if one could throw a dart across the entire universe and hit a bulls-eye one millimeter in diameter on the other side."[3] Certainly we can agree with David who said:

The heavens declare the glory of God;
    the skies proclaim the work of his hands. (Psalm 19:1)

Human Design

As a hand surgeon I am constantly reminded of the practical beauty of God's design. The very shape and form of the hand is a masterpiece of creation. When our fingers are stretched out, they spread apart like a fan so we can reach around an object. In this position they retain their flexibility to be able to wrap around a ball or to grasp a book. Yet when the fingers are curled into a grip or a fist, they close toward the center of the hand like the spokes of a wheel and become a rigid vice with little flexibility. This transformation is essential to the strength, stability and function of the hand.

The detail of the nerves of the hand is complex and breathtaking. Touching one point on the sensitive index finger skin will send electrical messages along a single cell from the fingertip to the spinal cord in the neck. A complex set of nerve connections then relays the electrical nerve impulse to a specific area of the brain. This signal is then converted into the release of a chemical to bring to our conscious mind, in a way not yet fully understood, the knowledge that we have been touched.

This incredibly detailed function is multiplied millions of times daily from all areas of our body, without us having to make one decision

[1]P. James E. Pebbles et al, "The Evolution of the Universe," *Scientific American*, February 1998.
[2]S. Weinberg, "Life in the Universe," *Scientific American*, October 1994.
[3]Gerald L. Schroeder, *The Science of God: The Convergence of Scientific and Biblical Wisdom* (New York: The Free Press, 1997).

to make it happen. Without this function, we could not tell where the various parts of our body are. Additionally, without the ability to sense pain, we could not survive. No machine has been able to match the complexity of this process. Truly,

> I praise you because I am fearfully and wonderfully made;
> your works are wonderful, I know that full well. (Psalm 139:14)

The strength of God's design leads us to humility. We have no cause for pride when we realize that God not only designed everything, but also brought it into being—without our help! Our response ought to be one of joy that we can serve the eternal God who designed and created the universe down to the last detail, yet cares about our smallest hurt.

Salvation's Design

God, the greatest designer, did not leave to chance the most important task we have on earth: He made his plan of salvation clear. God's perfect design involved the death of his Son on the cross and our response of gratitude, repentance and baptism (Acts 2:38).

While deciding to go to Cambodia to serve on the HOPE Worldwide team establishing a medical training and free-care hospital, one of the biggest challenges for me was giving up what I thought was control over my future and my financial security. Over and over again I have seen that it is God who is very much in control of his design. Our job is to be open to his will and to get on board with his plan.

> In his heart a man plans his course,
> but the Lord determines his steps. (Proverbs 16:9)

While we were preparing to leave Boston to move our family to Cambodia during 1997, fighting broke out in Phnom Penh. As we watched on the news programs the terrified faces of the Cambodians fleeing the city, we wondered if our going was really God's plan. Our faith was being tested. Had I followed my feelings and fears, we may not have gone. God's design became clear as one by one our very specific prayers were answered. For example, our house rented within hours of going on the market, vital surgical equipment was donated by a nearby hospital to be transported to Cambodia, and I saw God's protection over the team who were already in Phnom Penh.

When I accepted that God truly was the designer of the universe and was clearly the architect of the Sihanouk Hospital Center of HOPE in Phnom Penh, I gave my heart to his plan. We moved to Cambodia because I was convinced that God had a purpose and design for it all and would not neglect his children.

Since then God has blessed us incredibly. He provided for our housing requirements, provided suitable friends for our children at school and even met our children's specific dietary needs. By getting in line with God's design for us at this time, we were guaranteed an exciting life, a real opportunity to serve the poor, great friends, health and a good education for the children.

The God who created the universe and the intricacies of human anatomy has a plan for our lives as well. May we never cease to marvel at the ingenious designer who is responsible for it all!

God and You

1. When did you last look at creation and give praise to God for his great design? (Psalm 92:4-5).

2. How do you respond when people challenge the sovereignty of God? (Matthew 10:32).

3. What problems do you have that you feel are too small for God to worry about? (Matthew 10:29-31). How does an understanding of his intricate designs change this way of thinking?

4. How faithfully have you sought God's design for your life? (Matthew 6:33). Is there anything God could design for your life that you would not be prepared to do? (Matthew 7:21).

8

The Eye of the Beholder
A God of Beauty

GERI LAING
Durham, USA

Do you remember a time when you worked hard to create or beautify something? Perhaps you wrote something and got the words just right, or maybe you played to perfection a piece of music, or painted a lovely picture. Maybe it was a task as simple as cleaning a room, mowing a lawn or washing a car. Whatever the accomplishment, do you recall the sense of satisfaction and fulfillment you felt on its completion? There is something deeply gratifying about completing a job, and doing it right. In a *miniscule* way, this must be how God felt as he created the world, looked at it and "saw all that he had made, and it was very good" (Genesis 1:31). When I read the account of creation, especially of the first garden in Eden, it sounds so very beautiful. Try to envision the garden as it is described here:

> Now the Lord God had planted a garden in the east, in Eden; and there he put the man he had formed. And the Lord God made all kinds of trees grow out of the ground—trees that were *pleasing to the eye* and good for food...
> A river watering the garden flowed from Eden; from there it was separated into four headwaters. (Genesis 2:8-11, emphasis added)

Beautiful Creation

But beauty such as this was not limited only to Eden. Take a look around you! Look up into the skies—we see his beauty there. Look down into the depth of the seas—we see God's beauty. The beauty of our world inspires awe as it sings and shouts the glory of God, its maker.

> "See how the lilies of the field grow. They do not labor or spin. Yet I tell you that not even Solomon in all his splendor was dressed like one of these." (Matthew 6:28-29)

He has made everything beautiful in its time. (Ecclesiastes 3:11)

Creation is beautiful because its maker is a God of incomprehensible beauty. From the beginning, everything he made was a reflection not only of his mighty power, but also of his tremendous appreciation for what is lovely and beautiful. The beauty of our world is not accidental. God could have made a world that was much simpler: black and white, a level surface, no changes in climate or season, everything and every place exactly the same. The world still would have served his purposes and met our basic needs, but God chose instead to create a majestic, beautiful world that reflects his own glory.

Our earth was made quite methodically, one step at a time and with a huge amount of energy. Periodically, God stopped, stepped back and surveyed what he had accomplished and "saw that it was good." When he was done, God Almighty decided to rest. As he rested, God must have looked with sweet satisfaction upon his amazing creation. He had poured the best he had—indeed his very soul—into it, and the results were infinitely fulfilling. The world and its beauty were an expression of himself.

Thousands of years after his original creation, God was still concerned with beauty. When he instructed Moses and the Israelites to build the tabernacle (see Exodus 25-30), it is amazing how mindful he was to make it beautiful. It was not enough that it should be functional— he wanted it to be glorious!

If God cares so much and put such effort into making all things beautiful, what lessons are we to learn from this? First, we must open our eyes and see the magnificence of God all around us. When was the last time you saw a sunrise, really noticed a sunset or paid attention to the almost endless variety of birds, animals, plants and fish? When did you last thank God for all he made that shouts of his love, power and beauty?

But there is another lesson to be learned here, and we must pay attention to this one: Caring about beauty is not unspiritual, worldly or shallow! Of course Satan can fool us into concerning ourselves too much with outward appearances, ignoring the ugliness of sin that lies beneath. However, as a disciple, it is right and good—in fact, it is very much a part of God's nature and will—to notice and appreciate what is lovely and to care that things are "pleasing to the eye."

Beautiful Celebration

Not long ago we were involved in the planning of a very special wedding. It was a big celebration, a great event, and we wanted it to be beautiful. We spent months preparing for it, and we worked hard—very hard. The day of the wedding is a day I will never forget. I walked into our church building, and never had I seen it more beautifully arrayed. It was filled with flowers, greenery, candles, fabric and bows. My breath was taken away. It was beautiful beyond description, and I "saw that it was good." As the ceremony began, the music sounded as if we were a part of heaven itself. After the wedding, we went down to an outdoor pavilion where the reception was held. Again, it was glorious: Carolina blue sky, green grass, and—under the pavilion—more flowers, ribbons, fabric and bows. Everything was just as I had envisioned and dreamed it would be.

Why had we worked so hard? Why had we wanted it to be so special, so perfect? There were many reasons, but most of all because there was a beautiful young woman dressed in white silk who walked down the aisle that day. She was our precious daughter—the fruit of our lives together, the fulfillment of our dreams, hopes and desires—and yes, *years* of hard work. There was also a handsome young man dressed in a black tuxedo, whom we had come to love as our own son. These two young people pledged their lives and love together on that day, for as long as they both would live. We laughed, we cried and "it was very, very good."

Our God is a God of indescribable beauty and he expended tremendous energy creating a world for us, his children. Just as we wanted our daughter's wedding day to be wonderful and beautiful because we love her, so also God has created a breathtaking world just because he loves us more than anything he has made. He celebrates our lives; and every day, creation proclaims his undying love. He has surrounded us with beauty to enjoy, and to make us happy. Every sunset, every flower, every rainbow—all are created just so that God might see us smile.

Beauty is who God is, it is what he wants, and above all, it is an expression of his great love for us. Can we do anything less than deeply appreciate it and strive to reflect it in all we are and do?

God and You

1. *How have your own efforts to create or beautify something given you satisfaction?*

2. *What are some of the most beautiful things you have seen in God's creation? When did you last thank God for all he made that shouts of his love, power and beauty? When will you again?*

3. *Our lives as disciples are a reflection of God to the world. How are you doing in keeping yourself (1 Corinthians 6:19-20), your home and your surroundings in a state that pleases and reflects our God?*

4. *List two beautification projects you will commit before God to work on, and make sure to give yourself a deadline.*

9

He Alone Is Good

The Goodness of God

DEDE PETRE
Boston, USA

Give thanks to the Lord, for he is good;
  his love endures forever.

Psalm 118:1

Have you ever wondered how a bird knows how to build its nest? Early this spring, I watched every morning as a robin worked diligently to collect hay, grasses and twigs for a nest. Every day it would pull enough hay or grass to fill its beak, then fly to its tree to labor at weaving it all together. Not one of these days did I see this robin with another bird teaching it what to do. I asked my seven-year-old son about this as we watched the robin together one morning. He said, "Mom, God teaches birds these things, just like he teaches spiders how to build their webs." Well, there you have it. Kids make it simple, and it is: God in his goodness provides for the birds, insects and animals, just as Jesus said (Matthew 6:26).

Goodness Revealed

The knowledge and order in nature loudly proclaim that there is an ultimate power behind the universe that is entirely good rather than evil, loving rather than selfish, caring rather than aloof. Our God has provided an inherent knowledge to allow all species to protect and feed their young, to catch their prey, or to build their homes. Is this not amazing? Is this not a testimony to the goodness of God, as he provides for his creation? God cares. He provides all creatures, including humans, with all that we need. As Psalm 145 so beautifully puts it:

The Lord is faithful to all his promises
    and loving toward all he has made.
The Lord upholds all those who fall
    and lifts up all who are bowed down.
The eyes of all look to you,
    and you give them their food at the
    proper time.
You open your hand
    and satisfy the desires of every living thing.
(Psalm 145:13b-16)

Scriptures on the subject of God's goodness almost always carry
with them a sense of God's provision. His plan for survival is especially
detailed when it comes to the species created in his own image: man. By
giving us his word, God shows us how much he cares. Through the
Word, God provides for our survival! Consider these verses:

This is what the Lord says—
    your Redeemer, the Holy One of Israel:
"I am the Lord your God,
    who teaches you what is best for you,
    who directs you in the way you should go." (Isaiah 48:17)

[He] satisfies your desires with good things
    so that your youth is renewed like the eagle's. (Psalm 103:5)

You are good, and what you do is good;
    teach me your decrees. (Psalm 119:68)

The Lord is good to all;
    he has compassion on all he has made. (Psalm 145:9)

Goodness Personified

In his gospel, the apostle John refers to Jesus as "the Word." He
personified God's goodness! God cared that we would be fully provided for, so he sent his Son. Jesus once described God's goodness to
a somewhat naive young man:

"Why do you ask me about what is good?" Jesus replied. "There is only
One who is good. If you want to enter life, obey the commandments."
(Matthew 19:17)

Initially, we can take offense at this statement. *Hey, what do you mean, there is only one who is good?* We get confused on the issue of "only One," rather than seeking the true definition of "good." God's goodness, Jesus explained, is seen in his giving us a precise set of instructions for our lives.

On another occasion, Jesus explained to his followers: "I am the good shepherd. The good shepherd lays down his life for the sheep" (John 10:11). If a predator were to attack the sheep, the shepherd would throw himself in the way before allowing the sheep to be harmed. This, then, is the ultimate example of the goodness of God: Jesus on the cross. God provides. He gives us the means to be released from the bondage of sin. His goodness is abundant, constant, unselfish and beautifully displayed all around us.

Goodness Experienced

What does God's goodness mean to me? Everything. Over the years, through joy and pain, good times and hard times, his goodness has kept me humble, grateful and faithful. I must remind myself to look for his caring hand in the midst of the struggle. I have seen many different situations challenge my conviction that he will *always* provide what is best for me.

During my years as a leader in the singles ministry, I remember challenging sisters to write out lists of the characteristics of the man they would one day hope to marry. I myself wrote a list, prayed about it occasionally, and put it away in a folder. Later, as a young married woman on the staff of the Paris church, I rediscovered that list. Every characteristic I had written down was an exact description of my exceptional husband, Kelly. God had provided the perfect man for me!

As a young woman of fourteen, I vividly remember sitting at the bedside of my mother as she died. I prayed and believed that God would bring good from it; he did. Looking back, I can now see that this situation ultimately led me to become a Christian. Two years ago I sat at the bedside of my father as he died, and I had a hard time letting go. I grieved a long time for him, but the comfort and encouragement I received from God's word and my spiritual family helped me tremendously. I thank God every day for the many spiritual parents he has given me here in Boston. I also see how God used my father's illness to help my sister, Mary Ellen, become a Christian.

I especially thank God for his goodness in the area of discipling. God has always put "the right woman for the job" in my life to help me become more like Jesus. I am grateful for the ways each of these women has shaped my life. Bernadine Bellmor, who currently disciples me, has had an impact on my life beyond what I can express. I know I have grown and changed and matured so much under her leadership because of God's goodness and concern.

Genesis 22 sums up the story of the near-sacrifice of Isaac with these words: "On the mountain of the LORD it will be provided." Having seen God's goodness in an unmistakable way, Abraham called that place "The LORD Will Provide" (Genesis 22:14). Truly, all who understand the goodness of God claim that promise today.

God and You

1. Name some ways in which you see God's goodness displayed in nature around you.

2. Do you view God's instructions to us in his word as proof that he wants what is best for us? Or are his commands burdensome to you?

3. List some ways that you have seen God working for good in your life in joyful times and in challenging times.

4. Are there any situations now facing you that cause you to doubt God's goodness? Decide to change and to bring your perspective into harmony with what has been revealed to us in the Bible.

10

A Generous Heart
The Kindness of God

MARK TEMPLER
London, England

The Creator of the universe, clothed in power, is also kind in heart. While he could rule as a harsh tyrant, he instead displays kindness and concern at every turn:

> "But let him who boasts boast about this:
>   that he understands and knows me,
> that I am the Lord, who exercises kindness,
>   justice and righteousness on earth,
>   for in these I delight,"
> declares the Lord. (Jeremiah 9:24)

God's kindness began in the creation—he was good enough to give us life. Job 10:12 says, "You gave me life and showed me kindness." And God made a world where the needs of every creature are provided for abundantly:

> The earth is full of your creatures....
> These all look to you
>   to give them their food at the proper time.
> When you give it to them,
>   they gather it up;
> when you open your hand,
>   they are satisfied with good things. (Psalm 104:24, 27-28)

God Cares Deeply for His Creation

God is concerned about the hair on our heads, the beauty of the lilies, food for the birds and the life of a sparrow. When the mountain goat and the doe give birth, God counts the months till they bear and sees the labor pains of each (Job 39). He provided manna, quail and water for the

Israelites during their stay in the desert, and even made sure their clothes did not wear out (Deuteronomy 8). In Jonah 4, God mentions his concern for the cattle in Nineveh when he rebukes the prophet. And in John 2, Jesus provided the wine for a wedding feast when it had run out.

Nature is full of amazing symbiotic relationships. There are ants that live in trees, nourished by them and protecting them from predators. Lichens are formed by an alliance between algae and fungi. There are anemones who live on crabs, sharing the crab's food and stinging potential predators. There are birds that live alongside large mammals like the hippopotamus, eating the insects and parasites on their skin. It is amazing the way many flowers rely heavily on the bees and other insects who eat their nectar and spread their pollen, allowing them to reproduce. The universe around us is not some cosmic accident; rather, it reflects the creativity and kindness of our incredibly loving Maker.

God Cares Deeply for His Children

God's kind provision for us is evident in so many things that we take for granted. The earth is just the right distance from the sun—too close, and we'd burn; too far, and we'd freeze. Animals breathe out carbon dioxide, which is absorbed by plants and trees that give out oxygen, which animals can breathe! Mothers have breast milk as long as children need it, so even a poor child has a chance at good health. If we get injured, our bodies "know" how to heal themselves—wounds heal, blood clots, bones mend. In Paul's amazing sermon at Lystra he said:

> "Yet he has not left himself without testimony: He has shown kindness by giving you rain from heaven and crops in their seasons; he provides you with plenty of food and fills your hearts with joy." (Acts 14:17)

God has always led his people with kindness. The angels were kind to Lot (Genesis 19:19). God was kind to Abraham by getting a wife for Isaac (Genesis 24:27). Jacob prayed to God, acknowledging that he was unworthy of all his kindness (Genesis 32:10). God was kind to the midwives who saved the Hebrew firstborn (Exodus 1). He led the Israelites with "cords of human kindness" (Hosea 11:4). He was kind to David and his descendants (2 Samuel 22:51, 1 Kings 3:6), and showed kindness to the Jews in exile to Persia (Ezra 9:9). He is even kind to the angels (Zechariah 1).

Jesus taught that God is kind to the ungrateful and the wicked (Luke 6:35). Indeed, we can only be saved because of God's generous heart:

> But when the kindness and love of God our Savior appeared, he saved us, not because of righteous things we had done, but because of his mercy. (Titus 3:4-5)

Each of us has experienced God's kindness personally in many, many ways. We are alive. He takes care of our daily needs. He has offered us salvation. He has given many of us families. He has given us talents. And he even helps us in the small troubles of our lives.

A few months ago I wanted to visit a former disciple who had left the Lord and who later ended up in prison four hours from London. I neglected to make the needed appointment before boarding the train and rebuked myself once I had discovered my error. It was too late to turn back, so I prayed that God would be kind to me and my friend and that I could get in. After four entry refusals and subsequent prayers, I got in—because God is kind. The visit greatly encouraged my friend, and he will be restored to Christ soon. I walked away from the prison with an overwhelming sense of gratitude to God. I am sure you have had similar experiences in which God was kind to you. But the question for us is this: how should we react to God's kindness?

Don't Take God's Kindness for Granted

He is kind even to the wicked. Just because things are going well in your life, don't think that means God approves of your behavior. Paul warned the judgmental Jews:

> Or do you show contempt for the riches of his kindness, not realizing that God's kindness leads you toward repentance? (Romans 2:4)

Some disciples fall into persistent patterns of sin. When the sin does not immediately ruin their lives, they assume that in some way God approves of their behavior. But we must not mistake kindness and patience for approval of sin! Is there something you need to change, but have been putting off? The time has come to change it—today!

Be Kind Yourself

God is love, and God is kind. We must be kind. This is one area I have had to work at as a Christian. I am not kind by nature, but rather rude and impatient. But as I meditate on God's kindness, it makes me want to be kind to a world that does not deserve it—just as I do not deserve kindness from God. I appreciate so much the kindness I see in Christians around me, like my wife Nadine. Their example makes me want to be kind—like them and like my God.

Be Joyful and Grateful

God is extremely kind to his creatures. Some of us go through life filled with dark thoughts and a critical spirit. Our hearts are not filled with joy, but rather with bitterness, because we are not letting God's kindness touch our hearts. Thank God for his kindness in your prayers. Remember the many times he has been kind to you, and put a smile on your face!

God and You

1. Do you appreciate the kindness of God as expressed in nature? When was the last time you took some quiet time out to be surrounded by God's creation and to marvel at his kindness?

2. Do you thank God for the many small kindnesses he does for you, in providing you with food, clothing and a comfortable life?

3. Is God's kindness rubbing off on you? Are you kind?

4. Are you taking God's kindness for granted? Are there persistent, secret sins in your life?

GOD IN
PROVIDENCE

11
The Just Judge
The Justice of God

NICK YOUNG
Dallas, USA

How often have we seen people lose faith and be swept away by waves of despair, bitterness and even rage when they are seized with some great tragedy? As the storms of life rain sorrow upon their heads, they appeal repeatedly to the love and mercy of God for relief. If the tragedy abates and everything works out like they prayed it would, then they praise God for his grace and goodness. If, however, things don't go as they hoped, God's justice is called into question. But in all circumstances at all times, God is always just *and* always full of grace. Our judgment of his actions does not change that in any way. In times of great turmoil and crisis, it may not so much be a confidence in the love of God that we need, but an appreciation of the justice of God.

Part and Parcel

We may have few spiritual needs as great as our need to grasp the concept that God is just. Justice is as much a part of his character as holiness, mercy or love. Yet, divine justice is one of the least understood and most underappreciated qualities of God. You will, most likely, hear your preacher speak of the grace or compassion of God every Sunday.

On the other hand, the justice of the Lord may be mentioned only infrequently.

"Divine justice" refers to the fairness of God in his dealings with mankind. Unlike the gods portrayed in the literature of the world, the God of the Bible is perfectly equitable in the way he treats humanity. This concept is as fundamental and essential to God as any other moral attribute.

Loudly proclaimed in the Holy Scriptures is the concept that God is just. Notice the following passages with emphasis added:

He is the Rock, his works are perfect,
    and *all his ways are just.*
A faithful God who does no wrong,
    upright *and just is he.* (Deuteronomy 32:4)

"You came down on Mount Sinai; you spoke to them from heaven.
You gave them regulations and *laws that are just and right,* and
decrees and commands that are good." (Nehemiah 9:13)

He will judge the world in righteousness;
    he will govern the peoples *with justice.* (Psalm 9:8)

The Lord within her is righteous;
    he does no wrong.
Morning by morning *he dispenses his justice,*
    and every new day he does not fail,
    yet the unrighteous know no shame. (Zephaniah 3:5)

"Great and marvelous are your deeds, Lord God Almighty.
Just and true are your ways, King of the ages." (Revelation 15:3)

Ordinary Days

The justice of God can be seen in the ordinary days of our lives.
Jesus, in his Sermon on the Mount, called upon his disciples to love
their enemies. He attempted to motivate them to have that kind of heart
by reminding them of the character of God. He reminded them that the
Lord "causes his sun to rise on the evil and the good, and sends rain on
the righteous and the unrighteous" (Matthew 5:44-45). God's fairness
toward man stands both as our motivation and our model as we pursue
that same heart so that we may be sons of our Father in heaven.

Though it took many years for the apostle Peter to internalize this
message, he eventually declared:

"I now realize how true it is that God does not show favoritism, but
accepts men from every nation who fear him and do what is right."
(Acts 10:34-35)

Judgment Day

The justice of God will be ultimately displayed at the final judgment. The Bible describes a final reckoning that will be absolutely fair
and righteous:

[God's] righteous judgment will be revealed. God "will give to each person according to what he has done." To those who by persistence in doing good seek glory, honor and immortality, he will give eternal life. But for those who are self-seeking and who reject the truth and follow evil, there will be wrath and anger. There will be trouble and distress for every human being who does evil: first for the Jew, then for the Gentile; but glory, honor and peace for everyone who does good: first for the Jew, then for the Gentile. For God does not show favoritism. (Romans 2:5-11)

The reason we know that God's judgment is just is due to the fact that it is "based on truth" (Romans 2:2).

Your Days

The justice of God can make a real difference in the way we live. It can lead us away from sin. Accepting as fact that "God will bring every deed into judgment, including every hidden thing, whether it is good or evil" (Ecclesiastes 12:14), will certainly make a difference in our choices. Believing we will give an account to God for the way we live is the best deterrent anyone can have against sinning.

Knowing that God is just can also lead us to a heartfelt devotion. For the more we understand the justice of God, the more easily we will see the loving heart of God. Why does the Lord hold us accountable? It is not because he dislikes us or is angry with us or wants to deprive us of good. On the contrary, he reveals to us his justice because of his love, for he knows the effect such an awareness will have on us. We must persevere until we understand the ultimate realities that God is love, that he *always* wants what is best for us, and that in his justice this love is clearly portrayed. As a result, we will more naturally respond to him with loving devotion.

"Consider therefore the kindness and sternness of God," wrote Paul in Romans 11:22. The key word here is "and." Paul had just reminded his Gentile readers that the great mass of their Jewish contemporaries were rejected by the Lord due to their unbelief. At the same time, God had saved multitudes of former pagans like themselves. Paul called the Christians in Rome to take note of the two sides of God's nature that brought these situations into being:

Consider therefore the kindness and sternness of God: sternness to those who fell, but kindness to you, provided that you continue in his kindness. (Romans 11:22)

The disciples were to dwell not only on the goodness of God, but on his severity as well. They were to contemplate both qualities *together* in order that they might better understand each one individually.

Let us not fail to dig deep into the well of God's love, for therein lies the heart of the gospel that will sustain us through life. As we do that, let us also not hesitate to consider the justice of God, for it is equally important. Together they convey a picture of God complete enough to motivate any good-hearted soul to love and serve the Lord.

God and You

1. *How have you seen the justice of God in your life?*

2. *Do you truly believe that the Lord has treated you with perfect fairness throughout your life? Why?*

3. *How does the justice of God affect your motivation?*

4. *In what way will a better understanding of God's justice affect your heart? Your decisions? Your actions?*

12
Absolutely!
The God of Truth

FRANÇOIS AND PENNY FAURE
Paris, France

> Jesus answered, "...for this reason I was born, and for this I came into the world, to testify to the truth. Everyone on the side of truth listens to me."
> "What is truth?" Pilate asked.

> John 18:37-38

The world today echoes the words of Pilate in the first century: "What is truth?" For most people in our day, the idea of "truth" is a subjective concept: every individual can construct his own value system based on what seems best to him. As a result, people are left with the daunting task of figuring out, among countless possibilities, which ways are right and good for them in every area of life—what works for marriage, for training our children, for health, for our careers and for relationships.

We live in the age of "anything goes." It is not surprising that more and more people turn to science for answers, as it presents man as advancing and gaining seemingly more and more certainty about himself and the universe around him. In the realm of religion, the New Age Movement that claims so many adherents today teaches plainly that the truth is within each of us, there for the taking. Even modern Christian theology tells us that the Bible has as many possible interpretations as there are people willing to read it.

Sure and Certain

In sharp contrast with these modern doubts about truth, hear the bold affirmation of Jesus as he prayed to his Father: "Sanctify them by the truth; your word is truth" (John 17:17). God tells us plainly that truth exists—absolute truth—and that he gave it to us in his word.

Parents desire to develop confidence, trust, joy and security in their children's hearts. The key to these qualities is a total commitment to truth. God desires his children to experience the same thing. "Love," he says, "rejoices with the truth" (1 Corinthians 13:6). The psalmist describes it thus:

> Praise be to you, O Lord;
>   teach me your decrees....
> I rejoice in following your statutes
>   as one rejoices in great riches.
> I meditate on your precepts
>   and consider your ways.
> I delight in your decrees;
>   I will not neglect your word. (Psalm 119:12,14-16)

Do you still praise God like this for the privilege of knowing the truth? Do you still feel the joy and gratitude you first felt when you were set free by the truth? What a relief we felt when we finally allowed someone who was qualified—God—to begin leading our lives. No more groping along in the darkness! We remember, too, thinking "I don't deserve this" when we learned that God actually *wanted* to be our guide. Since that time, there has been an ever deepening sense of gratitude for God's truth which has been a lamp to our feet and a light for our path (Psalm 119:105).

Liar, Liar

Once when he was confronting a group of particularly deceived people, Jesus described to his antagonists the nature of Satan. Jesus warned them,

> "[The devil] was a murderer from the beginning, not holding to the truth, for there is no truth in him. When he lies, he speaks his native language, for he is a liar and the father of lies." (John 8:44)

Satan will always try to enslave us to sin again through his lies. When we let anything divert us from God's truth as defined in his word, we become easy prey for the ultimate liar.

We are especially vulnerable to these tactics when faced with failure, hurts or disappointment. When we are guilty of repeated sin, Satan tempts us to think: "It will get better tomorrow"; "Brother or sister X is in the same boat as I am"; "It's just not my strength"; or "They just don't understand my situation." We then become satisfied with little or no progress in our repentance, choosing neither to confess nor to seek help in overcoming these sins.

When someone hurts us or acts in a way that makes us feel uncomfortable, we can entertain critical thoughts toward them, assuming the worst, imagining that they have intentionally hurt us. We may be tempted to hold on to negative thoughts and feelings that ultimately estrange us from the person, without ever checking our assumptions against the facts or seeking help in resolving the conflict.

When facing circumstances that prompt strong feelings of loss, disappointment, sadness or loneliness, we may be tempted to allow these feelings to dominate our lives and our perspective. We may then accuse God of having deliberately caused these circumstances or of having abandoned us, instead of allowing him to comfort and encourage us through his word and the friendships he provides.

Truth Will Set You Free

God never wants us to remain in any of these situations. He has provided strong encouragement to us through the apostle Paul: "Finally, brothers, whatever is true, whatever is right...think about such things" (Philippians 4:8). Sanity and spirituality are restored only when we build our lives on what is real. "Stand firm then, with the belt of truth buckled around your waist" (Ephesians 6:14). Just as the wide, strong belt of a Roman soldier held all of his armor together, only our devotion to the truth will allow us to possess the qualities that make up the spiritual armor of God. We can stand firm when we take a stand for the truth.

About ten years ago, a friend of ours responded to the truth she saw in the Bible and decided to become a follower of Jesus. She has a genetic disease that causes intense migraines. Sadly, she is married to a man who neither respects her nor her commitment to God's truth. She also has three children, and she has always insisted on reading the Bible and praying with them at night, and taking them to church—even when it meant crossing half the city to get there. She has faced times of discouragement, but has never questioned God's faithfulness.

About a year ago, her oldest son was baptized. On Mother's Day, he shared about how his mother's steadfastness in the face of hardship convinced him to become a disciple. Her second child has expressed a desire to study the Bible. Her husband, after almost ten years of continual opposition, recently came to a marriage enrichment workshop and expressed his desire to learn more about the Bible. If she had bought into the lies that Satan threw at her for all those years, she would never have seen these victories.

As we face the challenges and the blessings of this life, we must never stop clinging to our God and the truth he has revealed. Only then will we experience what the truth alone can give—a life of real freedom.

God and You

1. *Do you ever entertain doubts about the truth of God's word in the Bible? God wants us to feel secure in his love. Satan is an accuser and deceiver.*

2. *Do you feel secure in your relationship with God, or are you regularly assailed by feelings of guilt and inadequacy? How can you permit God's truth to protect and strengthen you when Satan feeds you lies?*

3. *Take time to reflect on and write down examples of victories God has given you over insecurity, inadequacy and inappropriate guilt. Do you see God's providence and power in these examples?*

4. *Are you as grateful and refreshed by God's truth today as you were when you were a new Christian? Are you willing to do anything it takes to allow God's truth to bear fruit in your life?*

13

Straight A's
An All-Knowing God

NADINE TEMPLER
London, England

"Do you know how the clouds hang poised,
  those wonders of him who is perfect in knowledge?"

Job 37:16

To really know God is a challenge for every Christian. Yet God himself is perfect in knowledge—about us and about every aspect of creation, from the largest to the smallest. His knowledge transcends time and the limits of the human mind. It wraps itself around every aspect of creation. God knows all the intricate, minute details of the smallest particles and the biggest galaxies—even those whose existence is unknown to man.

As human beings, our view of the world is severely limited. It is difficult for us to see beyond our own little sphere of influence. Our knowledge is bound by the abilities of our own minds. Unfortunately, we assume that God is a lot like us—yet our minds cannot compare to his.

Man finds it hard to resist the temptation to belittle God and bring him down to his level. We see the unfortunate result—the creation of statues, idols and religious icons in many of the world faiths, including so-called "Christianity." This reduction of God makes us feel better about ourselves, makes us feel like we are in control. Our challenge is to surrender to a God who knows us immeasurably better than we will ever know him.

God Protects Us

God's absolute knowledge of absolutely everything can be either terrifying or comforting, depending on our perspective. "Does he not see my ways and count my every step?" (Job 31:4) The fact that God really knows all about us and our circumstances, added to the fact that God is perfect in his love and compassion, ought to produce tremendous comfort and security in us. He is looking out for us!

> You know when I sit and when I rise;
> you perceive my thoughts from afar.
> You discern my going out and my lying down;
> you are familiar with all my ways. (Psalm 139:2-3)

God knows our future too, so as long as we walk in his ways, there is really no need to worry. As a parent carefully watches his or her toddler's steps, so God protectively watches ours. When we feel misunderstood and the whole world seems to be against us, God knows our hearts. In fact, he understands us better than we understand ourselves!

What makes God's love and protection even more incredible is that he is perfectly aware of our sinful nature. He specializes in loving the sinners he created! Understanding God's knowledge of us should make his love for us more amazing still. Instead of being afraid of God, we can now feel secure that he knows us so well.

God's Judgment

On the other side of the coin is the fact that the all-knowing God is perfectly aware of our sins and weaknesses and will judge our hearts.

> Nothing in all creation is hidden from God's sight. Everything is uncovered and laid bare before the eyes of him to whom we must give account. (Hebrews 4:13)

We can hide from others around us, and sometimes we can even deceive ourselves, but we certainly cannot deceive God. God knows the real me. We can rationalize things away, yet God's judgment is perfect, made possible by his perfect knowledge. When we are face to face with God, everything is truly "laid bare."

God saw David's adultery before anyone else did; God knew Judas' heart long before the disciples did. Jacob deceived his earthly father, Isaac, but not his heavenly Father. Ananias and Sapphira could not fool God either. And God knew Job's heart far better than anyone, including Job himself.

We cannot run away or hide from God. We must repent right now or face the consequences. The first step is to be completely open and tell other disciples what you may be hiding, what God already knows, "for God is greater than our hearts, and he knows everything" (1 John 3:20).

One of the women in my ministry had been a Christian for a few years and yet had never really blossomed. She led a Bible Talk, but did not seem "free" and excited about her life. Something seemed to be holding her back. Every time she was challenged on her lack of zeal, she would nod, smile and agree, but she did not change.

Finally, after a discipleship group on openness, she confessed to having been immoral soon after her baptism. She had hidden her sin from other Christians, and it had robbed her of her joy. This sister totally repented and her joy level soared as she experienced a freedom she had not felt since her baptism! I am happy to say that she is on the ministry staff now and doing very well. However, it would have been much better for all concerned if she had realized earlier that God knew her sin and there was no point in hiding from him.

God's Knowledge Makes Us Humble

The other realization we must come to as we consider God's knowledge is our proper place in the creation. God's mind is so perfect, we should stand in awe of it.

"For my thoughts are not your thoughts,
    neither are your ways my ways,"
            declares the Lord.
"As the heavens are higher than the earth,
    so are my ways higher than your ways
    and my thoughts than your thoughts." (Isaiah 55:8-9)

If any of us ever start to feel proud of our intellectual achievements, our education or even our spiritual insights, let us make sure we keep things in perspective. The wisest and most learned man's knowledge is like a tiny drop compared to the ocean of God's mind.

This should not be a discouraging thought; it should instead open our eyes to our need for God. When we don't have the answers to problems or questions, we don't have to feel helpless. We may never fathom all mysteries; but God does, and he is in control.

God's knowledge raises the issue of control. I came from a nonbelieving background in which education and intellectual pursuits were an end in themselves. I spent many agonizing years searching for the truth. It was such a relief to find God! Perfect knowledge belongs to God and not to me. I had to relinquish control and accept that I will never have all the answers to life's questions. The fact that God does is good enough for me. To be aware of the limitations of our imperfect minds keeps us humble.

Others of us were raised believing in an all-knowing God, yet the paradox lies in the fact that we still try to control the amount we disclose to this all-knowing God. Even though we have always believed in him, we still have not totally surrendered our lives to him. This must change.

Let's remember who we are and who God is. As we do, let's share about him with a world that does not understand the satisfaction of surrendering to an all-knowing, loving Creator!

God and You

1. *The all-knowing God sees you. Are you open about your life with other disciples? When was the last time you resisted temptation because you were aware of God's presence?*

2. *Have you surrendered your future to God, or are you still trying to be in control of your life? What circumstances tempt you to take back control?*

3. *What are you tempted to worry and fret about? How will you turn these areas over to the God who knows and understands you better than you do?*

4. *How does the knowledge of God influence your daily life?*

14

High and Holy
The Holiness of God

ONYECHI OGUAGHA
Lagos, Nigeria

I saw the Lord seated on a throne, high and exalted, and the train of his robe filled the temple. Above him were seraphs, each with six wings: With two wings they covered their faces, with two they covered their feet, and with two they were flying. And they were calling to one another:

"Holy, holy, holy is the LORD Almighty;
the whole earth is full of his glory."

At the sound of their voices the doorposts and thresholds shook and the temple was filled with smoke. "Woe to me!" I cried. "I am ruined! For I am a man of unclean lips, and I live among a people of unclean lips, and my eyes have seen the King, the LORD Almighty."

Isaiah 6:1-5

We can talk about the different qualities of God and be utterly amazed. God is awesome, powerful, almighty, great, most worthy of praise! He is incomparable. He is the only God. There is no one before him or after him. He is the King Eternal. As great as these attributes are, it was another quality of God that made Isaiah, one of the most spiritual soldiers of the Most High, cringe in fear and reverence. God stands alone in his holiness.

In a Class by Himself

God is without any flaw or blemish. It is absolutely impossible for him to commit sin. He cannot even be tempted by evil (James 1:13). There is nothing in the nature of God on which sinful men can lay blame. He cannot tolerate the presence of the sins that wage war against our souls for even a fleeting instant. He has never sinned and never will. He is incorruptible. He sits exalted, high above any other throne or dominion, absolutely pure and without flaw. He is the Lord Almighty and "holy is his name"! (Luke 1:49).

The great prophet Isaiah, when faced with just a meager glimpse of God's holy perfection, felt utterly ruined. Isaiah did not see God per se, for no one can see the holy one of Israel and live. He saw a glimpse of his dominion. Anybody with an iota of human reason or sensitivity would feel absolutely inadequate and ruined. And it would not matter how spiritual you thought you were. Even the heavenly beings in Isaiah's vision covered their faces and feet before the throne of the LORD, shaking the temple in song as they praised him for his holiness. God's holiness is simply *awesome*, in the original meaning of this overused word.

Writing this chapter is extremely humbling for me. I feel like Isaiah—unworthy, sinful, unclean hands, unclean lips, utterly ruined—because a sinful wretch like me is trying to describe the holiness of God. As I write this, all my sins and mistakes come crashing to the forefront of my mind. The deceitful things I have said and done that hurt God, my family and other people really help me to understand that whatever grain of righteousness I have is due to God's mercy. Compared to him,

> All of us have become like one who is unclean,
>   and all our righteous acts are like filthy rags;
> we all shrivel up like a leaf,
>   and like the wind our sins sweep us away. (Isaiah 64:6)

God is so holy that he could not look at his one and only Son hanging on that horrible cross, carrying my sin and yours upon him. When Jesus cried out in heart wrenching agony and pain, "My God, my God, why have you forsaken me?" (Matthew 27:46), God's holiness would not permit him to look or respond. This kind of holiness defies description.

The Call to Imitate

> But just as he who called you is holy, so be holy in all you do; for it is written: "Be holy, because I am holy." (1 Peter 1:15-16)

God calls us to be holy because he, God, is holy. Now you are thinking, "How is this possible, considering what we just examined?" It is required in strong terms that every true disciple of Jesus strive for perfection. Though we can never attain God's level of holiness, we are nonetheless called to give it our best shot! Jesus' death on the cross has completely purchased our salvation; we can never be saved by our own efforts. But looking to our heavenly Father's example, we must genuinely desire to "be imitators of God, therefore, as dearly loved children" (Ephesians 5:1). With fervent prayer and fasting, we must endeavor with all our might to be holy.

As clear as the Biblical call to imitation is, we often fail to really practice it. Mike Taliaferro, who leads the effort to evangelize Africa, is my hero. I have the rare privilege of being discipled by him. He loves God and is a great imitator of God and godly men. To my shame I confess that I have not always been like him in this area. There are times that my pride and defensiveness toward him has hurt the church I lead in Lagos. The result of second-guessing him has been to reap just what I sowed: The men that I disciple in the Lagos church developed the same attitude toward me. It was scary!

In recent months, God opposed my ministry and me because of my know-it-all attitude. (See 1 Peter 5:5.) I felt horrible and alarmed at how bad my heart had gotten. I had not been a good imitator, and my pride had put a wedge between me and one of the best of men. Thankfully, God is gracious. He has given me a second chance, and I am being refreshed because I made a decision to repent. What about you? Are you being a good imitator of the spiritual people God has put in your life? We must never stop imitating the godliness we see in our leaders.

The Call to Persevere

God expects us to be like him. We have no excuses for not living up to his expectations. We will fall sometimes—this comes with the territory. And we will not fully attain perfection in this life. Rather, this is a training ground to prepare us for eternal life with our God. Our labor and our quest to be like God will not be in vain.

The way of holiness is not easy. If we are to succeed, we must hold on to God's promise:

Let us not become weary in doing good, for at the proper time we will reap a harvest if we do not give up. (Galatians 6:9)

Are you tempted to quit in your desire to be like God in his holiness? Look at the harvest that awaits those who do not give up. We can all strive to imitate the holiness of God. He expects us to. An abundant harvest of joy and peace awaits us when we do. Isn't that what the Christian life is all about?

God and You

1. Have you ever blamed God for your problems? Was God really responsible, or was it your own sinful desires?

2. As a disciple with sinful lips and hands, what posture do you assume in your heart before a holy God? Are you like Isaiah, or are you proud?

3. How much have you prayed and fasted for God to give you the power to imitate his holiness? Have you resisted the call to imitate? Can you feel God's opposition?

4. In which area(s) have you fallen short of God's standard of holiness? What excuses have you made for not attaining to it? How will you change?

15

Nobody Does It Better

The Perfection of God

KAREN LOUIS
Singapore

He is the Rock, his works are perfect,
　　and all his ways are just.
A faithful God who does no wrong,
　　upright and just is he.

Deuteronomy 32:4

God is perfect! He is complete in everything and lacking in nothing. His word is perfect; his ways are perfect; even his thoughts are perfect! A mere attempt to consider the perfection of God's creation as presented in Part 1 of this book staggers the imagination. Yet the flawlessness of God goes beyond his acts of creation; he is perfect in all he is and does.

Couldn't Be Better

The Bible is full of verses that explicitly mention God's perfection:

- God's *will* is perfect (Romans 12:2).
- God's *knowledge* is perfect (Job 36:4).
- God's *ways* are perfect (Psalm 18:30).
- God's *word* is perfect (Psalm 19:7).
- God's *faithfulness* is perfect (Isaiah 25:1-3).
- God's *gifts* are perfect (James 1:17).

What's exciting is that these are not just some theological platitudes we can hang on our walls or type on our screensavers—these truths about God's perfection need to change our attitudes about God and our relationship with him forever.

Since God's *will* is perfect, the goal of our lives needs to be discovering that perfect will for us. We can trust him even when nothing seems to be going right, because he makes no mistakes. As long as we are living in his will, we can know that things are happening for a reason (Romans 8:28).

Since God's *knowledge* is perfect, we must remember that God knows all of our sin perfectly (ouch!), so there is no use trying to hide from him. Our best bet is to be open with God and with others who can help us as we "aim for perfection" (2 Corinthians 13:11).

Similarly, since God's *ways* are perfect, and we know that ours are not, we should not be offended when well-meaning friends point out our weaknesses and rebuke us for our sin. In fact we should treasure the people in our lives who love us enough to help us become "perfect in Christ"! (Colossians 1:28-29).

Since God's *word* is perfect, we need to make the best use of our time to read it, study it, learn it, meditate on it and live by it. If we look "intently into the perfect law that gives freedom," we will be blessed (James 1:25).

Since God's *faithfulness* is perfect, we can totally trust him when he says we are saved and our sins are forgiven. Insecurity with God is an insult (1 John 5:13).

Since God's *gifts* are perfect, we should be grateful for the gifts God has given us and not be envious of what has been given to others (i.e. looks, personality, intellect, talent, money, education or spouse). Discontent, ingratitude and jealousy were killers in Bible times, and they are killers today (James 3:13-18).

All About Character

Obviously, trying to comprehend all of this can be a bit daunting. Therefore, in order for us earthlings to even be able to relate to God's faultlessness and completeness, let us focus on just one of the many facets of his perfection: his character.

How perfect is God's character? Think of some Christians you know whom you respect. As exceptional as they are, you undoubtedly see at least a few weaknesses in their character. Normally, those weaknesses are in areas related to their strengths. For instance, a brother who is a great servant might also struggle with being a people-pleaser. A sister who is a strong leader might also struggle with impatience. But God does not have this problem. His character is flawless and perfectly well rounded.

Since the Bible says that all the fullness of deity dwells in Christ (Colossians 2:9), let's look at Jesus' life to see the perfection of God's character. Jesus was tender and loving, yet not sentimental; zealous and fearless, but also wise and cautious. He was relatable, yet not worldly; confident, but not arrogant. Jesus was obviously self-sacrificing, but at the same time joyful. He was urgent and responsible, yet peaceful and unhurried. God's Son was always under attack, but always composed. He was strong and uncompromising, yet not harsh. God in the flesh was dignified and authoritative, yet humble; respected and revered, yet approachable. He was a strong leader of men, but also a man of prayer and a servant of servants. This description is not meant to be exhaustive, but we can very well become exhausted just trying to comprehend it!

In Need of Perfecting

This understanding of the character of God became particularly important to me several years ago. Although I felt like my strengths lay in the areas of sensitivity and encouragement, I was being told by several reliable sources that I needed to improve in the area of speaking the truth in love to others. When left to my own sinful nature, I am a sentimental, people-pleasing, conflict-avoiding coward who almost gets around to saying something! In my arrogance, I prided myself in how Christlike I was—so patient, compassionate and "loving"—yet I was completely blind to my need for change, despite the urgings of my husband and friends. Sadly, as a leader, this meant that I was not having the impact I needed to have on the women around me.

Finally, a true friend of mine told me, "Karen, you think you've got the balance of Christ in dealing with people, but you don't! You are not eager to imitate the parts of God's character that are not your natural strengths, like his indignation, his forthrightness and his expectations. You must desire to imitate God in *all* areas if you want to have Christ's perfect balance!" Scales fell from my eyes, and I was finally able to "get it." God has helped me to continue to change in this area, as I follow the One with the perfect character.

Even though we may never truly grasp God's perfection, we can certainly stand in awe of him, and we can join in with David's victory song from Psalm 18:

As for God, his way is perfect;
    the word of the Lord is flawless....
It is God who arms me with strength
    and makes my way perfect. (Psalm 18:30, 32)

God and You

1. *Why should an understanding of God's perfection be an encouragement to us?*

2. *Which area of God's perfection discussed here stirs your heart the most? Why?*

3. *What character trait do you have that you think of as being Christlike? What are some corresponding weaknesses?*

4. *Who do you have involved in your life, inspiring you in your relationship with God and helping you to be perfect in Christ?*

16

It's Under Control
The Sovereignty of God

RON DRABOT
Charlotte, USA

Who can speak and have it happen
   if the Lord has not decreed it?
Is it not from the mouth of the Most High
   that both calamities and good things come?

Lamentations 3:37-38

Julie (not her real name) woke with a start and sat up in bed. Something was wrong. The twenty-eight-year-old Virginia Tech student lived alone in a cabin located in a remote area outside of Blacksburg, Virginia. She and her boyfriend had been dating for six years. He was usually a warm and sensitive guy; but that night, as he got out of his truck, Julie realized that something was not right. He was very drunk.

Once inside the cabin, he went to the dresser in Julie's bedroom where he knew she kept a loaded handgun for protection. Taking it out, he began to threaten her. Suddenly he came toward Julie and pointed the gun at her head. Screaming, she fell to the floor in front of him. She heard the blast of the gun. She lifted her head to a scene of absolute horror. At the last moment, he had turned the gun on himself. He died instantly.

Theresa stepped out into the rain in front of the Pterodactyl Club in Charlotte, North Carolina. It was 3:15 AM, and she was just leaving a masquerade party at the city's hottest nightspot, dressed as Cleopatra. Saying goodbye to her friends, she ran to her car. After putting her belongings in the trunk, she turned around to find herself confronted by a man with a gun. He demanded her money. Theresa handed him her purse and then made a decision that would change the rest of her life. On her key chain, she had a small mace canister. She sprayed her assailant in the face. Unaffected by the chemical, he put the gun to her head and shot her at point blank range through the right eye. The twenty-one-year-old UNCC student was left lying face down on the pavement.

Tragedy. Unexplained, unexpected, senseless tragedy. It happens all the time. To the unspiritual mind, life is a giant game of roulette. Spin the wheel and hope for the best—but never forget that around every corner may be tremendous success or hopeless horror. Not so for the disciple of Jesus. We trust a God who is absolutely sovereign and in total control. However, *knowing* that God is in control leaves two compelling questions that every man and woman must face.

Is God Trustworthy?

Can God be trusted? Is there any purpose or reason for all the events that occur in our lives? Will he be there to catch us? The gap between intellectual knowledge and an unqualified trust in God can only be bridged by personal experience. The Scriptures are clear. The psalmist wrote,

> "Call upon me in the day of trouble;
>   I will deliver you, and you will honor me." (Psalm 50:15)

God does not promise his people freedom from adversity. He does, however, guarantee that every event in our lives is used for his purposes and for our ultimate good:

> And we know that in all things God works for the good of those who love him, who have been called according to his purpose. (Romans 8:28)

God's control is constant and not sporadic. Psalm 31:15 tells us that our times are in his hands. Often it is only later that we come to see the purpose and wisdom of God.

Eleven years after the tragedy at the cabin, "Julie" was met by a disciple in Charlotte, North Carolina. She lived blocks away from my wife, Lavonia, and me. After studying with us, Julie and her husband were baptized into Christ in the summer of 1998. God's eternal purpose was working long before she knew or acknowledged his presence.

Can I Trust God?

The bigger challenge is not whether or not *God* can be trusted, but rather, can *I* trust God?

They spoke against God, saying,
   "Can God spread a table in the desert?
When he struck the rock, water gushed out,
   and streams flowed abundantly.
But can he also give us food?
   Can he supply meat for his people?"
When the Lord heard them, he was very angry;
   his fire broke out against Jacob,
   and his wrath rose against Israel,
for they did not believe in God
   or trust in his deliverance. (Psalm 78:19-22)

Though it was a miracle that she was even alive, Theresa, who had been shot in the head, awoke from her three-and-a-half-day coma unable to walk, talk or eat. She was totally paralyzed. Thirty days after being shot, she moved her leg for the first time. Months later, Theresa defied the laws of physics and the predictions of her doctors to take her first awkward steps. In December of 1998, twenty-seven-year-old Theresa Vera walked unassisted down the aisle with her fellow graduates at the University of North Carolina at Charlotte.

Theresa Vera could see no earthly reason why she was blindsided by a tragedy at the age of twenty-one. She had every intention of becoming a lawyer. Years after the accident, as she painstakingly worked her way through the remainder of her degree, another student on the UNCC campus invited her to a Bible talk. After studying the Bible, all of the events of her life came into focus. God's hand had been moving, even through tragedy. Looking back, Theresa says, "Without the intense challenges that I have endured, I never would have been humble enough to even attend church or become a disciple of Jesus."

On a personal note, in 1990, when our firstborn son died on the mission field, I could not understand how God would use this for his purposes. When he was buried in Syracuse, New York, my sister Diane (who had been an atheist for most of her life) attended the funeral. Soon the seeds of faith that were planted by the disciples she met there began to grow. As a result of his death, a church was planted in Syracuse sooner than originally planned. And seven years after Joshua's death, Diane was baptized as a disciple of Jesus. I could not help but remember the words of Hezekiah: "Surely it was for my benefit that I suffered such anguish" (Isaiah 38:17).

God does not tell us *why* he allows adversity. He does not explain it to us! Even Job was never told why he was allowed to go through what he did. We do know that Satan's role in the drama seems to slip into oblivion. Satan is never mentioned again after the first two chapters of Job. God is the one who powerfully works his plan for each of our lives.

God and You

1. In what area have you resisted trusting God?

2. Why do you find it difficult to trust him in this area?

3. What concrete changes can you make today in order to totally surrender yourself to the will of God in this area?

4. What will be the result of total trust in his sovereignty?

GOD IN REDEMPTION

17

He Stoops Down
The Condescension of God

STEVE ROSENBAUM
Boston, USA

You stoop down to make me great.

Psalm 18:35

March 25, 1996, was a day I will never forget. My wife, Kathy, and I trembled in nervous awe as we awaited a most special meeting in the lobby of the Jianghan Hotel in Wuhan, China. We had labored for more than three years and traveled to the other side of the planet. Ten other American couples were there for the same purpose. Through the caring efforts of the Hope for Children adoption agency, all ten couples were poised to adopt orphaned little girls into our families.

Then *the moment* came. Our name was called, and an orphanage director placed her in my wife's arms—a six-month-old, eight-pound gift of life named Huang Fu Yin. We took her up to our room and cried. That day she was reborn as Natalie Kate Rosenbaum. We gave her the first bath of her life and carefully peeled the cradle cap from her delicate head. She refused our offers of formula at first, but was soon gulping down whole bottles!

Later that night, several of the adoptive fathers gathered to pray for our new daughters. Before each dad prayed, he shared the circumstances under which his respective daughter had been abandoned and then how she had been brought to an orphanage. It proved to be a lesson in salvation so powerful that we all wept as each realized the greatness of what God had done.

The seemingly endless paperwork, the financial sacrifice and the disappointment of deferred departure dates—all of these are now precious memories we would not want to change a bit. Natalie and her new big brother, Nicolas, are our most treasured possessions on earth. (Read Deuteronomy 14:2.)

Eager to Adopt

This experience epitomizes for me the idea of the condescension of God. For untold ages before any of us were born, our Father in heaven did some elaborate family planning, carefully thinking through a multitude of spiritual adoptions. To prepare a home for us, the Almighty created the amazing physical universe we live in (Genesis 1-2). Then for centuries, our Creator sent prophet after prophet to reveal his family plan (Hebrews 1:1-3).

Ultimately, when it came time to pay for the actual adoption of our souls—God came himself. It is the ultimate lesson in personal responsibility. No prophet would do. Not even a mighty archangel. Who would undertake such a costly task?

> But when the time had fully come, God sent his Son, born of a woman, born under law. (Galatians 4:4)

Descending from a throne, with dominion over all creation, came Jesus Christ, who "being in very nature God, did not consider equality with God something to be grasped, but made himself nothing" (Philippians 2:6-7).

Do we, as free members of God's household, even begin to conceive of how much our Father in heaven radically altered his own comfortable existence in order to free our souls from bondage? I'm talking about God's own willingness to come down to our level. You see, for a perfect heavenly Dad to win the hearts of hardened, worldly, runaway kids, he decided to become one of us. Can you imagine the cost-counting conversation in heaven as the Father explained to the Son that he must be made like them in every way? (Hebrews 2:17).

John 1:14 reveals, "The Word became flesh and made his dwelling among us." The Crown Prince of Creation left his eternally secure place at God's right hand, where he had equality with God, and took the very nature of mortal man. From infinite to finite. From Sovereign to subject. From omnipotent to needing food and drink to survive. From Creator to created. Are we as blind to the wonder of Christ's entry into our world as the innkeeper who banished Mary and Joseph to a barn to give birth to God?

No longer would angels worship at his feet. In Joseph's home, the agent of creation learned carpentry at his earthly father's feet. This is the irony of ironies: the Creator being taught by the created how to create! The Teacher spent years allowing himself to be taught—at home and in the synagogue. How many hundreds of hypocritical sermons did the Righteous One have to endure, while resisting the temptation to be silently critical?

God's House Has Many Rooms

What can all this mean for you and me, practically? First, allow the heroic example of God in Jesus to inspire your own willingness to make sacrifices as you strive to "become all things to all men" (1 Corinthians 9:22). And second, ask yourself, "What kind of commitment am I really willing to make to the lost around me?" Most disciples are willing to verbally share their faith with just about anyone from any walk of life, but what about truly befriending people? Spending a lot of our precious time with them? Building a lifelong friendship with them? Honestly, we usually make that kind of commitment only with people who are like ourselves. Imagine if Jesus took that approach in his outreach to us—he would never have left heaven!

How willing are you white-collared professionals to not only associate with people of "low position," but to humble yourself, serve and win their hearts? Are you, "Mr. Blue Collar Tough Guy," willing to crucify your worldly resentment of those higher up the economic ladder so as to win their respect and then their souls? I pray to God that we may never see the day when it is an exception to find disciples willing to change their lives, schedules, personalities and even cultures to win souls.

To what extent should I be willing to change? We need only ask: To what extent was Jesus willing to change? The answer is, the cross. At Calvary we see not only the brutal execution of an innocent man, but we see the Son of God once again undergoing a radical transformation—of the darkest kind. God's family plan of salvation would not be complete without the destruction of sin in our lives:

> God made him who had no sin to be sin for us, so that in him we might become the righteousness of God. (2 Corinthians 5:21)

The harsh reality of this passage conveys that for Jesus to die for sinners, he had to "become" one. On the cross, he who was holy "became" sin. It was as though the Truth became a liar in order to die for all of our deceit. It was as though the Giver of Life became a thief, as though the Faithful One became an adulterer. He who had defined unconditional love absorbed into his soul history's crimes of hate.

The Father could respond to this horrific display of sin in only one way: to have no relationship to it—even when it involved his own offspring. At the cross, God showed his willingness to go to any length to pave the way for a relationship with us.

Truly, God placed no limits on his condescension in an effort to reach you and me. To what extent are we willing to go in order to reach a lost world?

God and You

1. Does your prayer life reflect an awareness of the intensity of God's outreach?

2. What can you do to improve your study of God's word that would reflect an attitude of seeing the Bible as a love letter from God, as opposed to it being "required reading" for a disciple?

3. Who are you winning to Christ?

4. What do you need to change in order to win that person?

18

The Gift Giver
The Grace and Mercy of God

Tammy Fleming
Moscow, Russia

Amazing grace. Infinite mercy. Isn't it strange that these words, which should evoke a deep response of joy and should stir up a flood of gratitude, often breeze by us, barely skimming the surface of our hearts? We should be astounded. We should be overcome with wonder and thanksgiving. *God, help me shake off the sinful numbness and worldliness of my flesh and help me to appreciate you as you deserve!* Living in the material world day in and day out makes it difficult for us to stay in tune with how startling these gifts of grace and mercy really are. I once wrote a song about this:

> Here in the city, we kind of forget where we are.
> We can't contemplate a mountain; we can't see the stars.
> Here in the city, we live in a mess of towering steel.
> It gets so we don't trust anything, but what we can touch
> and feel.

And yet, the most important things in our lives are absolutely the unseen things. Love. Peace. Friendship. Salvation. Eternity.

Consider the act of baptism. Baptism is a powerful statement of belief in a whole slew of miracles which are unseen, culminating with our contacting the blood shed on a cross by our merciful Lord two thousand years ago! How bizarre that there is no thunder, no lightning, no earthquake, no angelic proclamation shouted from the clouds. In fact, after baptism we return to the same familiar situations at home, the same old physical bodies, the same troublesome emotions. And yet an earth-shattering change has taken place—invisibly.

From Death to Life

Satan tempts us in many ways to trust the tangible things in this world and to doubt our faith, thereby making the essential concepts of grace and mercy fall with a lifeless thud on hard hearts. A dangerous example of this is how we easily forget that we were truly and hopelessly dead in our sins—and we *deserved* to be dead:

> As for you, you were dead in your transgressions and sins, in which you used to live when you followed the ways of this world and of the ruler of the kingdom of the air, the spirit who is now at work in those who are disobedient. All of us also lived among them at one time, gratifying the cravings of our sinful nature and following its desires and thoughts. Like the rest, we were by nature objects of wrath. But because of his great love for us, God, who is rich in mercy, made us alive with Christ even when we were dead in transgressions—it is by grace you have been saved. (Ephesians 2:1-5)
>
> Offer yourselves to God, as those who have been brought from death to life. (Romans 6:13)

When we forget that we were dead in our sins (the bad news), we will certainly fail to appreciate God's gracious gift of salvation (the good news).

Two nights ago at the beginning of our church service, my friend and I had a moment of heart-stopping panic. We had momentarily lost track of her toddler and realized with a shock how easily he could have fallen from the nearby second story window to his death on the pavement below. When we located him in the next few seconds, alive and toddling around contentedly, we both felt an incredible rush of relief and gratitude, which is just too sweet for words. In our hearts, he had been brought from death to life! This is just what God's grace and mercy will produce in me if I am spiritual enough to stay in touch with it.

Trusting in Grace, Not Appearances

Recently, I spent the evening with a student named Tanya. She had come to Moscow from a poor family in distant Magnetogorsk and had been met by disciples and invited to study the Bible. She joyfully gave her whole life to God with great zeal and became a Christian. God's grace was evident in all of this. Now, six months later, almost every measurable aspect of her life seems worse than before. Her roommate regularly brings her boyfriend home to spend the night with her in Tanya's presence and persecutes Tanya for her new faith. She cannot find a job, and therefore cannot send money home to help her parents, a fact which worries her and makes her feel terribly guilty. She also cannot pay next semester's tuition at the music academy, which means she could lose her place at the school and her place to live in Moscow. Did something change? Did grace run out?

Tanya needs to remember that no matter how things look on the surface, God's grace and mercy are *always* working powerfully in her life backstage, hidden from view—for now. As Romans 5:1-2a teaches, she has already gained access to God's grace and is standing in it. What's more, the scripture continues,

> We rejoice in the hope of the glory of God. Not only so, but we also rejoice in our sufferings, because we know that suffering produces perseverance; perseverance, character; and character, hope. And hope does not disappoint us, because God has poured out his love into our hearts by the Holy Spirit, whom he has given us. (Romans 5:2b-5)

Life as a disciple gives us a real spiritual purpose and ambition: to become more like Jesus every day. Who knows, perhaps these current difficulties have been especially allowed by God in order to refine her character. A Christlike character is what she will need to achieve her most precious dream—the hope of attaining heaven herself and taking all those dear to her along with her. You see, God's mercy is always at work in his purposes. Besides, as for Tanya—she was dead! It's just great to be alive again.

Satan is so cruel. He would love for us to think that God lured us into the kingdom on some pretense and now has no intention of fulfilling his promises to us. With our earthbound, mortal vision, we have not yet learned to see with God's eternal perspective. We can start to focus on the disappointments around us and doubt God's goodness. And yet the Scriptures are clear:

> God our Savior...wants all men to be saved and to come to a knowledge of the truth. (1 Timothy 2:4)

> God does not show favoritism. (Romans 2:11)

He will have mercy on *all* of us, and what a miracle this is! Not one of us deserves it. Each of us is so wicked that nothing we ever do could make up for our sins—truly, we were dead. Yet God's incredible grace and mercy are lavished on us, according to his great pleasure (Ephesians 1:5-8), in order that we might know God and have fellowship with him forever.

God and You

1. *What is your general attitude and posture toward your salvation? Do you feel unworthy and indebted to God's grace, or are you numb to the tremendous gift you have received?*

2. *When you talk about your conversion, do you describe your sin clearly, so that your listeners sense the amazing grace and mercy of God in opening the door of the kingdom to you (and, therefore, to them)?*

3. *Have you put any conditions on your relationship with God, doubting your standing with him until you see some particular situation change?*

4. *God's designs for our lives are based on mercy and grace. How can it help you to have this perspective when times are hard?*

19

I'll Be Waiting
The Patience of God

Sunny Chan
Hong Kong

The Lord is not slow in keeping his promise, as some understand slowness. He is patient with you, not wanting anyone to perish, but everyone to come to repentance.

2 Peter 3:9

Bear in mind that our Lord's patience means salvation, just as our dear brother Paul also wrote you with the wisdom that God gave him.

2 Peter 3:15

The apostle Peter, in the above passages, urged his fellow Christians to consider one of the outstanding character traits of God: his patience. In the *Oxford English Dictionary*, "patience" is defined as the power of enduring trouble, suffering or inconvenience, without complaining; the ability to wait for results, to deal with problems calmly.

There came a time in the first century when trials became very real to the disciples. They were persecuted by the Roman government (1 Peter 4:12). They were tempted to go back to their former religious tradition, Judaism, and tempted by false teachings that had more appeal to them than the truth (2 Peter 2:1). They were enticed by the sins of worldliness and lust (1 Peter 4:3-4). Some of them began to agree with and side with scoffers (2 Peter 3:3), doubting that Jesus would keep his promises. Others complained that God was too slow in bringing about justice.

It seems unbelievable that the first century Christians, having witnessed the miracles and great things that Jesus and his apostles had done, still lost their patience in the face of trouble, suffering and inconvenience. But this was nothing new. The same thing had happened in earlier generations. When Moses brought the Israelites out of Egypt, they saw miracles and experienced protection from the hand of God, but they, too, were impatient. They grumbled so much that God finally decided not to let them enter the promised land.

Rush, Rush, Rush

Human beings are impatient creatures. We prize quick results and quick fixes. Relationships between men and women break down because people lack the patience to build them properly, wanting instead to immediately enjoy all their benefits. As a result, divorce and broken relationships are all around us. Sadly, there are even Christians who lose their faith when faced with difficulties.

Not so with our God. God is patient. He has a plan for the human race, including the men and women he created who have doubted or forsaken him. He promised offspring beyond number to Abraham when Abraham was not yet convinced of his destiny. He promised Moses a land flowing with milk and honey, even when Moses wanted to quit. He sent his only son Jesus as a sacrifice to free us from our sins, as he had promised long ago, even when our response to him was mockery and hatred.

Jesus endured trouble, suffering and inconvenience—and always emerged victorious. God does not simply reside and reign from above, ignorant of what is happening to us. He is patient because he has experienced the trials of this life firsthand. His eyes are always fixed on our salvation, our eternal relationship with him. No matter how harsh or inconvenient the situation, how great the suffering or how hard our hearts become, he makes plans to help us change. He waited seventy-five years to call Abraham and eighty years for Moses. He walked all the way with Abraham and made him the father of the faithful, a true friend of God. He accompanied Moses to mold him into a man of conviction and a leader with great strength and great love for the people. And he waited for just the right time to send Jesus, the Savior of the world.

Patient Dreams

The earliest trace of Christianity in China dates to AD 635. However, it died out very soon. During the Ming and Ching Dynasties

(AD 1550-1911), many missionaries came to China, but few peoples' lives really changed. Even today, the government has so much control over religion that Christianity is difficult for people to understand and practice. But God is patient with the Chinese, and he has a plan.

One hundred years ago the British took over Hong Kong. It became well known in the world as a center of free trade. My generation's parents came from the mainland, but we ourselves were born and raised in a free country, sheltered from war and poverty. We were educated mostly in schools built by the early missionaries, hearing of God and Jesus from our infancy.

In 1987 a group of seventeen disciples was sent from Boston to Hong Kong. Led by Scott and Lynne Green, they began to preach the gospel to the Chinese people. The church grew rapidly, and ten years later, it numbered 1,850 disciples. Not only did the word of God spread in Hong Kong, but a group of powerful Chinese leaders were raised up and trained. In July 1997, Hong Kong returned to China. This meant the return of two thousand disciples to this formerly unconquerable land to spread the good news of Jesus. In 1999, an unprecedented ten thousand people attended the church in Hong Kong. Truly God has great plans in store for this nation of 1.6 billion souls, over one-fifth of the planet's population!

God is a God of victory, but he waits patiently. In the past twelve years, we have witnessed thousands of Chinese men and women break away from tradition, from fear and from sin, and be baptized into Christ. We have seen disciples locked up in jail, expelled from the country and harassed by the police; but they still hold firmly to Christ, share their faith, study the Bible with others and serve the people around them. It's all because they have learned from God to endure trouble, suffering and inconvenience.

We must learn to be patient, brothers and sisters, because God is patient. He has a plan for you, for your neighborhood and for your country. Let us not focus on our troubles, hardships and inconveniences, but learn from him to care for the salvation of the people around us. Let us be cheerful and full of faith toward our family members and friends—even when they reject and dislike us. And let us, through prayer and the study of God's word, strengthen ourselves to be patient like God. In the words of the Hebrew writer:

Let us fix our eyes on Jesus, the author and perfecter of our faith, who for the joy set before him endured the cross, scorning its shame, and sat down at the right hand of the throne of God. Consider him who endured such opposition from sinful men, so that you will not grow weary and lose heart. (Hebrews 12:2-3)

God and You

1. *What can make you lose your patience easily, and what can you do about it?*

2. *On a scale of one to ten, how patient are you toward your family members? Your parents? Your spouse? Your children? How could you be more patient with them?*

3. *Do you see how patient God is toward you and the people in your country? Can you see his plan for you and your country?*

4. *Have you given up on God in any area of your life, due to impatience? How will you repent?*

20

In Harm's Way

Our Refuge and Protector

LIN BEATY
Fairfield, Conn., USA

Blindness of glaring sun, steel on steel, darkness. Crimson blood, sirens, blue flashing lights. Confusion. Fear. I was eighteen years old when I was involved in my first automobile accident. I remember the jumble of emotions as blood rolled down my face. Above everything else, I remember the amazingly calm and gentle voice of my mother reading in the midst of my tears,

> God is our refuge and strength,
>   an ever-present help in trouble.
> Therefore we will not fear, though the earth give way.
> (Psalm 46:1-2)

She read until my heart was at peace. Little did I know then how many times I would turn to this scripture in tears and read until, once again, my heart was surrendered and at peace.

Many Storms

It is easy to praise God and preach on his goodness, protection and love when we feel shielded by him from life's storms. Our faith, however, is neither exposed nor refined through calm times. Only when the tempests of life assault us do we see who we really are, what our faith is made of, and ultimately, who God really is.

The winds of hardship began blowing in my life at the young age of eight. I was a prisoner of war for three months during a communist coup in a Latin American country. I will never forget the tanks, the bombs, the deaths. The overriding memory in my heart, however, is of my mother's calm surrender. I can still hear her singing "Jesus Loves Me" to us as we lay huddled with her and as she swatted away the flies from our faces. I remember her teaching us to be thankful daily. Our prayers were simple: "Thank you, God, that the bombs didn't fall into the flower garden today." I never doubted that we would be rescued and freed because of her belief that "God is our refuge and strength." He saved me and brought me through it stronger and more full of gratitude and faith.

At age twenty-seven, I married the man of my dreams and moved to New York City to train in the ministry with Lisa Johnson, the woman I longed to be like. Life seemed great until, once again, the waves came crashing in. My husband, Barry, was diagnosed with a brain tumor and was given five years to live. Mercifully, twelve years passed with no sign of reoccurrence. Then in December 1997, another brain tumor was found—and this time Barry was given only one year to live. What seemed like a countless series of storms followed one right after the other—my mom's breast cancer, my dad's rapid degeneration from Parkinson's disease, the deaths of three other relatives, my son starting to have seizures, being monitored myself for breast cancer, and on and on. I was left feeling out of breath spiritually, and afraid and faithless. If God was my strength, why did I feel so weak?

In the months that followed, I came to realize that Satan had used these storms of life to tear at my relationship with God. I studied the Psalms and was amazed by David's honesty with God and how he was able to work through his emotions in difficult times. I studied the book of Job and saw how unspiritual I was. I studied Second Chronicles and saw the victory of those who relied on God and the defeat of those who did not. Through it all, I was supported, discipled and encouraged by Cynthia Powell and Debbie Wright, women of intense faith and deeply spiritual lives.

The time had come for me to dig down deep. My roots were too shallow to withstand all these storms. It was time to throw away my self-reliance and get back to the humility of a surrendered, dependent relationship with God. The difficulties of that period of my life taught me several life-changing lessons.

God Is Still God

It was time to recall that God is God and that he is enough. He is, always has been and always will be in control. Psalm 46:10 reads, "Be still, and know that I am God." In stillness, I understood that God's comfort (2 Corinthians 1:3-7) and protection (1 Corinthians 10:12-13) were forming a gentle hedge around me. It made me cry to think of all the people in the world who go through storms in life alone—without the support of the kingdom and without an understanding of God's discipling. I believe with all my heart that God has used every difficulty in my life to cause my roots to go deeper, to make my heart truly spiritual and to refine my faith. He is the great discipler.

My Home Is Heaven

I feel ashamed of my shortsightedness when I hear Paul referring to the intense struggles of his life as "light and momentary afflictions" (2 Corinthians 4:17-18). Time and again I would think about my heroes—Deborah, Joseph, David, Daniel, Paul—and their amazing courage in adversity. They simply loved to please God! Paul and the first century disciples clung to the hope of a heavenly reward, eagerly looking forward to it. I had become too bound to the earth to dream of heaven. Looking forward to heaven makes my struggles worthwhile. They are part of God's way of getting me there. Placed in this eternal perspective, storms lose their power to overwhelm.

Righteousness Is My Goal

We must make it our goal to please God (2 Corinthians 5:6-10). At one point during my struggle, my goal was to simply make it through—not to grow and change, not to please him. I committed to start praying that God would be proud of me and that I would not miss one of the lessons he wanted me to learn. He was faithful. He exposed my sin and brought my heart to repentance and righteousness.

Righteousness means thankfulness. In 1 Thessalonians 5:18 Paul says, "Give thanks in all circumstances." I started thanking God and was amazed at how gratitude breeds gratitude.

Righteousness means surrender. Jesus in Mark 14:36 shows us to pray, "not what I will, but what you will." God has a great plan for my life (Jeremiah 29:11) and my heart needs to wrestle until it is surrendered to his will.

Righteousness means humility and dependence on God, not self-reliance (2 Chronicles 20:12). Each day does have enough trouble of its own, but God has more than enough strength to provide for us.

God has been my refuge and protector through all of these storms. Barry is recuperating well after a year and a half, with no signs of tumor reoccurrence.

> Who shall separate us from the love of Christ? Shall trouble or hardship or persecution or famine or nakedness or danger or sword? (Romans 8:35)

Shall revolutions, brain tumors, cancer, seizures, fears or spiritual struggles?

> No, in all these things we are more than conquerors through him who loved us. (Romans 8:37)

God and You

1. *What scripture do you turn to the most when storms hit your life? If you don't have one, ask some friends what their favorite passage is, and then choose your own.*

2. *What did you learn from the last major trial that you went through? Who will you teach this lesson to?*

3. *When was the last time you thought about heaven?*

4. *Who helped you through a difficult time recently? Have you expressed your gratitude to them?*

21

Unfailing Love
God Is Love

JOHN REUS
Sao Paulo, Brazil

Ana discovered six months ago that she has cancer. She is in a battle for her life, yet I have never seen her more joyful. When I mentioned this to her, she replied, "I have decided to see God in my life." The apostle Paul, commenting on God's love, challenges us to "know this love that surpasses knowledge" (Ephesians 3:19). If we are going to know God, we must know and experience his love, because "God is love" (1 John 4:8).

God's Love Declared

The Bible is full of declarations of love. God pours out his heart to us. Listen:

"I will betroth you to me forever;
　　I will betroth you in righteousness and justice,
　　in love and compassion." (Hosea 2:19)

How great is the love the Father has lavished on us, that we should be called children of God! And that is what we are! (1 John 3:1)

God proclaims his love for you, but like Ana, you must *decide* to see it. So often we struggle with doubts and discouragement because we have not trained the eyes of our hearts to spot the countless ways that God is pouring out his love on our behalf. Ana *decided* to see God's love in her life in the midst of physical pain and an uncertain future. And you? Are you actively searching for the daily examples of God's love in your life and all around you? Do you believe God as he declares his love to you? Are you listening?

God's Love Shared

"God sets the lonely in families" (Psalm 68:6). God's love has moved him to put us into an environment where his love can be experienced daily. Read Ephesians 3:14-21. As we are "rooted and established" in an environment of love, we will certainly grow in our understanding of his love.

Claudinei left family and friends to live and work in São Paulo. One month later he was adopted into God's family. Recently, his appendix ruptured, landing him in a public hospital to undergo two surgeries, suffer an infection, and occupy a cot in a recovery room with twenty other patients for twenty-nine days. Every day the Christians were there to encourage him and meet his needs. While the other patients received few, if any, visitors, Claudinei had a literal waiting list of brothers and sisters. Even as I write, he is living it up as he continues to recuperate at our home. I guarantee you that his understanding of God's love has deepened!

God is constantly revealing his love for us through the church—through friendship, discipling, encouragement, support, concern, etc. How sad it is to see some who view the church as an obligation or inconvenience, who are critical and complaining at times. I hope you will not need a trip to the hospital (or worse) to recognize how much God loves you and how he strives to show you his love through his church. It is in that loving family, "together with all the saints," that we will grow in our knowledge of God's great love for us.

God's Love Reproduced

God wants us to hear about his love. He wants us to see and feel his love being poured out all around us. And he wants to reproduce that same love within us! As a young Christian, I remember being frustrated while trying to understand and be motivated by the love of God. Then it dawned on me that I was struggling to understand God's love because I, myself, was struggling to love. I was not making much of an effort to imitate the love of Christ—I was still too dominated by my selfishness. I had been personally involved in bringing few people to Christ and I was causing little impact in the lives of other Christians. I repented. Then I began to see, up close, God's love touching and changing the lives of others.

How exciting it is to see God's love working through us! It lights up our relationship with him, filling us with admiration and thanksgiving. It's amazing to think about the people whose lives God has allowed us to touch, to see the fruit of his love in their lives, and to receive in return the spiritual rewards of gratitude and eternal friendship.

Read 1 John 4:7-12. God wants us to know his love by reproducing it in our own lives. Are you striving to imitate Christ's love? If you are, you will most certainly grow in your understanding and insight into God's love for you.

God's Love Received

Two years ago, Ronaldo was finishing his studies at the best university in Brazil. He was graduating number one in his class, the pride of his family, with job offers and invitations to graduate school. From all outward appearances, the future looked great...but he had decided to commit suicide. On the inside, life was empty; sin weighed heavily. He was tired at twenty-two years of age. The plan was almost perfect. For two months he was going to put everything in order, leaving money for funeral expenses, distancing himself from friends and family, and then, on April 25, it was all going to be over.

One detail had been overlooked, however—Fernando's insistence that Ronaldo study the Bible with him. Three weeks later, Ronaldo was rejoicing in God's love, forgiveness and purpose. Today he is a fast-growing intern on the ministry staff, grateful to the God who loves him so much that he sent his own Son to die in his place.

No other expression of God's love is so enthusiastically heralded in Scripture as is his love in the redemption and salvation of sinners. Read Romans 5:6-11 and Ephesians 2:1-10. How can God make the intensity of his love for us any clearer? The barriers are broken down and his arms are opened wide.

> I will praise you, O Lord my God, with all my heart;
>> I will glorify your name forever.
> For great is your love toward me;
>> you have delivered me from the depths of the grave.
> (Psalm 86:12-13)

God's Love Returned

> "I have loved you with an everlasting love;
>> I have drawn you with loving-kindness." (Jeremiah 31:3)

Why is it so important to God that I know how much he loves me? Because he wants his love returned. He wants to see the fruit of his love in our lives—hearts full of gratitude, longing to draw near, to obey, to please, to sacrifice, to persevere—hearts yearning for the day when we will know completely the love of God.

God and You

1. *How often do you take time to meditate on God's expressions of love for you? Write down ten ways God has demonstrated his love for you this week and specifically thank him in prayer for these.*

2. *How loving are you perceived to be by those around you (at home, church, work, school, etc.)? What decisions do you need to make that will enable God's love to have a greater impact in others' lives through you? What do you need to change?*

3. *Who are the Christians you know who seem to have a deeper understanding of God's love? Write down their names and initiate some great fellowship with them.*

4. *Without a doubt, the sharing of our faith helps us grow in our appreciation of God's love (see Philemon 6). Share in detail about your conversion with some non-Christian friends this week.*

THREE IN ONE

22
There Can Be Only One
The Uniqueness of God

ANNE-BRIGITTE TALIAFERRO
Johannesburg, South Africa

"O Lord, God of Israel, there is no God like you in heaven above or on earth below—you who keep your covenant of love with your servants who continue wholeheartedly in your way."

1 Kings 8:23

We are impressed by things that are unique: the Mona Lisa, the pyramids, *Star Wars*, the Empire State Building. As exceptional as they are, these things can be compared to other works of man, but in our God we find one who is truly unique.

"To whom will you compare me?
Or who is my equal?" says the Holy One. (Isaiah 40:25)

God is the incomparable one, and when we look at numerous passages of Scripture that describe God's uniqueness, they seem designed to produce awe and worship. They appear as strong reminders for us to let God be God and not to try making him in our image. How is God unique? Let's look carefully, and then stand in awe.

God Doesn't Change

"I the Lord do not change." (Malachi 3:6)

Every good and perfect gift is from above, coming down from the Father of the heavenly lights, who does not change like shifting shadows. (James 1:17)

Often we can think that God changes like we do. Our emotions and thoughts can wrongly lead us to believe that God isn't listening; that maybe he doesn't like us anymore; or even that the rules may have changed without our knowing it. Isn't this how we are? We become insecure in our relationship with the Father because we think that he acts like we do.

A roller coaster ride best describes how we can be in our faith at times: up and down, sometimes several times a day. We may feel like sharing our faith or we may not. We are happy and then not happy. The encouraging truth is that God does not and cannot change.

God's Unique Love

"I led them with cords of human kindness,
    with ties of love;
I lifted the yoke from their neck
    and bent down to feed them." (Hosea 11:4)

For God so loved the world that he gave his one and only Son, that whoever believes in him shall not perish but have eternal life.
(John 3:16)

God's love is unlike any other love. Some of us are more comfortable with that than others. We all feel a certain responsibility when we understand that we are deeply loved. There are expectations. There are hopes. None of us likes to disappoint people. Some of us feel that if we can make God out to be a little less loving, it becomes easier to not meet his expectations for our lives. We lower the standard and think that God won't mind. We continue in sin, not dealing with how it hurts God. The flip side of our misunderstanding of his unique love is when we imagine God's love is so magnanimous that it allows us to sin without consequence. We set up a false god of tolerance that has nothing to do with the real God and his real love. God's unique love demands wholehearted devotion and repentance from us.

God's Unique Strength

Who is this King of glory?
    The Lord strong and mighty,
    the Lord mighty in battle. (Psalm 24:8)

"God is mighty, but does not despise men;
    he is mighty, and firm in his purpose." (Job 36:5)

What happens when we forget who God is and what he can do? We complain; we make excuses for ourselves; we become ungrateful. In Job 32, Elihu rebuked Job for justifying his own attitudes and complaints, and for not acknowledging God's sovereign strength. But honestly, when was the last time something difficult happened in your life and you sought to justify God? We lose sight so easily of God's strength. We seek strength from our jobs, our families, our accomplishments—or even our religion. We think that these things will sustain us and forget that it is God who sustains. Elihu was right about one thing:

"If it were his intention
    and he withdrew his spirit and breath,
all mankind would perish together
    and man would return to the dust." (Job 34:14-15)

What do you complain about? Do you ever feel that God has somehow forgotten you or your requests? In Isaiah 40 our complaining is corrected as we are reminded that God does not grow tired or weary. Unlike us, God's strength is unique and unlimited! In our impatience for God to act according to our timetable, we must never doubt his ability to act powerfully for our good.

No Other God

Acknowledge and take to heart this day that the Lord is God in heaven above and on the earth below. There is no other. (Deuteronomy 4:39)

Therefore since we are God's offspring, *we should not think* that the divine being is like gold or silver or stone—an image made by man's design and skill. In the past God overlooked such ignorance, but now he commands all people everywhere to repent. (Acts 17:29-30, emphasis added)

Iyabo Akin-Lewis was raised in Nigeria. Her religious upbringing was a melting pot of Islam, African tribal religion and mainstream denominationalism. God, the one true God, was an afterthought, a being only approached or appeased by other gods or witch doctors. Sacrifices were offered to various gods (the god of fire or iron or the river) at the family shrine in the home of her grandfather.

Iyabo began visiting a traditionalist, or witch doctor, when she was thirteen years old. The reasons for the visits were usually centered around protection from enemies, from dreams or even from the future. Often when protection was needed, the witch doctor would appeal to the supreme being or god of the ancestors. Iyabo's husband, Akin, remembers visiting the cemetery as part of their wedding ceremony in order to "meet" and bow down to her ancestors.

Early in her marriage, after suffering two miscarriages, Iyabo turned to tribal religion to solve the problem. The traditionalist gave her concoctions to eat, made twenty-one incisions on her body from head to toe, and told her to not take a bath for three days! When this did not work, she looked to Islam, the religion of her mother. The Muslim "alfas" or priest would write down verses of the Koran with chalk, wash it off into a bowl and have Iyabo drink the mixture to ensure the promise of fertility. Even in false Christian religion, witchcraft and gospel were mixed.

Iyabo's life was forever changed when she became a true disciple of Jesus Christ and found the one true God. She realized that God wanted a relationship with her. He wanted her to talk directly to him—there was no need for the false gods and intermediaries. Only God had the power to change her life, the God she could approach without fear and without any barriers.

Are you growing in your love and understanding of the one living God? Long after the world forgets there was a Mona Lisa, pyramids or *Star Wars*, God will still be in heaven, unique and like no other god that we can devise.

God and You

1. *Why is it good to just be amazed at God and stand in awe of his incomparable qualities?*

2. *How have you been insecure in your relationship with God? In what areas can God's unchanging nature make you secure?*

3. *How do you view God's love? What changes does God's love encourage you to make?*

4. *What do you complain about? How can God's unique strength help you?*

23

We Three
The Trinity

DOUGLAS JACOBY
Washington, D.C., USA

When considering the miracle that took place when God became man in the person of Jesus Christ, the apostle Paul exclaimed, "Beyond all question, the mystery of godliness is great" (1 Timothy 3:16). These words could as easily apply to the Biblical doctrine of the trinity. Indeed, as C. S. Lewis noted, the trinity is not the sort of doctrine inventors of religions would concoct, which is one reason it may have the ring of truth to it! Believers in the early Christian era spent generations hammering out the doctrine of the trinity, investigating the intricacies of the Spirit. And though the term "trinity" is not in the Bible, the doctrine it describes gives as good an explanation of the nature of the godhead as anything man has come up with.

What Is the Trinity?

The Oxford English Dictionary (OED) defines trinity as "being three; group of three. From Latin *trinitas,* 'triad.'" Surely the Father, the Son and the Holy Spirit are not distinct persons as are the Three Musketeers, the Three Tenors or the Three Little Pigs. On the other hand, we are not simply dealing with one person in three roles, like a woman who functions as mother, wife and professional. The first error to be avoided is tritheism—three separate gods; the second is modalism—in which God "morphs" from one form to another, according to the need of the hour.

To understand this doctrine, we must first grasp what theologians mean when they discuss the "persons" of the trinity. In modern English "three persons" strongly implies a triad of gods. But the theological term "person" is from the Latin *persona,* which means "mask, part, character," as in the characters of a play. This of course does not mean that God is somehow "pretending," like an actor.

In brief, the holy trinity is the three-in-one.

Biblical Basis

Often the Father, Son and Spirit are mentioned together in the New Testament:

May the grace of the Lord Jesus Christ, and the love of God, and the fellowship of the Holy Spirit be with you all. (2 Corinthians 13:14)

Therefore go and make disciples of all nations, baptizing them in the name of the Father and of the Son and of the Holy Spirit. (Matthew 28:19)

They are three in personality but one in nature or essence. Father, Son and Spirit are each God (in essence), but none can be identified with the other. In short, all three persons are divine.

Obviously, our heavenly Father is God.

In addition, many verses state that Christ is divine (2 Peter 1:1, Titus 2:13, John 1:1, 14), not to mention the indirect proofs of his deity, such as his forgiveness of man's sins (Mark 2) and claiming as his own the name of God (John 8:58). But how can Christ have two natures simultaneously? An illustration may help. Lemonade is one hundred percent wet, and yet it is also one hundred percent citrus. It is not somehow half wet and half citrus—it's wholly both at the same time. In the same way, Jesus is human *and* God.

Finally, it is also clear from the Scriptures that the Spirit, the third person of the trinity, is divine. According to the OED, the Spirit is: "the active essence or essential power of the Deity, conceived as a creative, animating or inspiring influence." Now this may be an accurate definition, but how does it help us be closer to God? It makes a difference in our lives only when we sense and appreciate that God, through his Spirit, is living within us (John 14). The Spirit in nature is God; all members of the trinity are equally divine.

An Analogy

No single analogy adequately captures the divine mystery, though various illustrations are more or less helpful to different people. To explain the relations among the persons of the trinity, I most often use the analogy of the amorphous forms of H_2O. As seen in the illustration below, ice = water, liquid water = water, and steam = water (in essence); but ice ≠ steam, ice ≠ liquid water, and liquid water ≠ steam. Similarly, the Father, Son and Spirit are all God, but we cannot correctly say that the Father is the Son, or that Spirit and Son are interchangeable.

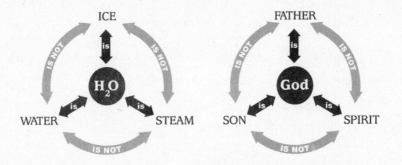

I like the water analogy, but its shortcoming, if taken too far, is that it implies the false doctrine of modalism—that God appears in one form now, another at another time. I have heard weaker analogies: comparing God to time (past, present and future), even to an egg (shell, white and yolk). The truth is that God is *unique*, so his nature can never fully lend itself to simple comparisons.

Trinity and Our Walk with God

The real power of the doctrine of the trinity lies in the ways it can illuminate our walk with the Lord.

First, the trinity brings us great assurance. The Father is God above us, the Son is God beside us, and the Spirit is God within us.

Second, the trinity helps us to see that God is love. How could God have been eternally loving if he had no one to love? The answer is, as Augustine and others have surmised, that love has *always* existed among the members of the trinity. The three-in-one God is a divine family, in which perfect love has always been exchanged.

Third, respect for the trinity deepens our humility, compelling us to accept God's transcendence. As Isaiah learned, there is an unfathomable distance between his ways and wisdom and our own (Isaiah 55:8-9).

If the whole thing seems complicated, don't fret! Theologians struggled for centuries to put the divine mystery into words; if you cannot manage it in half an hour, I wouldn't be too concerned! God cannot be put in a box, so this little chapter is certainly not the last word on the subject. His nature is a mystery—and so we will always have to strive to our utmost to embrace and accept the nature of God in our lives.

During the Restoration Movement of the nineteenth century, there was a reaction against trinitarian language. The closing words of the famous hymn "Holy, Holy, Holy" were changed to "God over all and blessed eternally." Yet it is wholly unnecessary to distance ourselves from the original wording of the song. Its final verse spoke the truth perfectly well:

Holy, holy, holy! Lord God Almighty!
    All thy works shall praise thy name,
    in earth, and sky, and sea;
Holy, holy, holy! Merciful and mighty!
    God in three persons, blessèd Trinity!

God and You

1. *In your prayers, do you jump indiscriminately from Father to Son to Spirit, or do you have a sensitive appreciation of the various persons of the trinity: praying in Jesus' name through the power of the Spirit to your Father in heaven?*

2. *Can you think of any other analogies that illustrate the trinity?*

3. *How often do unbelievers ask you about the doctrine of the trinity? Are you striving to become more competent to offer helpful answers to sincere questions?*

4. *In what ways will a deeper understanding of God's true nature affect your walk with him this week?*

24
Abba, Father
God, the Father

JANET FLEURANT
Nairobi, Kenya

"I will be a Father to you,
>   and you will be my sons and daughters,"
> says the Lord Almighty.

2 Corinthians 6:18

Recently we flew from our new home in Nairobi, Kenya, to encourage the brothers and sisters in Abidjan, Ivory Coast, where we had lived for the last eight years. En route, as I thought about my spiritual family, I began pondering the significance of having the Almighty God as my Father. Some of us are blessed to have had fathers growing up who were very loving and very much involved in our lives. Others of us either grew up without a father, or with one who was less than what we would have hoped for. It is comforting to know that whatever experiences we have had growing up, we can *all* enjoy the incredible privilege of having the Creator of heaven and earth as our Dad.

I was blessed with a wonderful father growing up. As with most things in life, it was not until I got older that I really began to appreciate what I had. Throughout my childhood, my dad was very involved in my life. He was someone I could always talk to, someone who helped me to believe I could do anything I set my mind to, and perhaps most importantly, someone who was not too proud to acknowledge his mistakes and apologize to me when he was wrong.

For those of us who were blessed with attentive, caring fathers, we must be careful not to take our relationship with God for granted. For those who did not have this kind of father, the challenge is to build your concept of who God is purely from the Bible, not giving in to the temptation of thinking that God is like your earthly father.

The Perfect Father

How would you describe the perfect father? What would be his attributes? If I were to formulate in my mind the perfect father, here are just a few of the important qualities I would include.

Good fathers pay attention to their children. Psalm 139 beautifully describes the intimate interest our heavenly Father takes in each one of us. But not only is he interested, he also wants to meet our needs. Jesus confidently assures us of this in Matthew 6:31-33.

Children with caring, protective fathers feel free to run to them in all different circumstances. David's psalms show how he poured out his physical, emotional and spiritual needs to God. For example, he cried out for protection from his enemies and leapt for joy when God came through (Psalm 28:7). During one particularly trying time, he exclaimed, "Free me from my anguish" (Psalm 25:17). And acknowledging his Father's wisdom and power, David often went to him for advice (Psalm 5:8).

A good father cares deeply for his children and wants them to be successful. God expresses his desire that his people be successful in every area of their lives (see Deuteronomy 30:9). He also carefully leads us through all the different phases of our spiritual growth:

"It was I who taught Ephraim to walk,
    taking them by the arms....
I led them with cords of human kindness,
    with ties of love;
I lifted the yoke from their neck
    and bent down to feed them." (Hosea 11:3-4)

God is all this and much, much more! He is truly the perfect Father for whom we all long.

God's Discipline

We have all had human fathers who disciplined us and we respected them for it. How much more should we submit to the Father of our spirits and live! Our fathers disciplined us for a little while as they thought best; but God disciplines us for our good, that we may share

in his holiness. No discipline seems pleasant at the time, but painful.
Later on, however, it produces a harvest of righteousness and peace
for those who have been trained by it. (Hebrews 12:9-11)

The Bible tells us that like all good fathers, God disciplines us.
Growing up with a father who was a major in the Air Force, discipline
was not a foreign concept in our household. Though at times I struggled
to see the purpose for it, I grew to understand that my father's discipline
was indeed for my good. Now that I myself am a parent of three children
whom I love more than words can express (Daniel, 7; Sahai, 5; and
David, 3), I realize that there are many things that my children would
love to do and would like to have that are just not good for them. Like
any children, they struggle with being told no. But I know that, one day
when they get older, they will understand. Discipline is basically God
saying no, and stopping us in our tracks. It is not pleasant and we do not
always like it, but we desperately need it.

Without discipline we would remain immature, spoiled children
who never quite grow up—always demanding our way. We must learn
to respond correctly to God's discipline. We cannot ignore it, nor can we
allow ourselves to become discouraged by it. Rather, we must respond
in a mature manner, like the psalmist did in Psalm 119. He used to
wander off until God disciplined him; but then he closely followed God's
word (v67). He realized that the suffering God sent him was good for
him, teaching him to pay attention to God's principles (v71). He also
discovered that God's decisions are fair and that he was disciplined
because he needed it (v75).

When God disciplines those he loves, he is treating us as his sons and
daughters (Hebrews 12:6-7). He uses his word, hardships and people
around us to help us in our walk with him. I have learned to appreciate
people who help me to keep things simple, like Anne-Brigitte Taliaferro.
Over the years, she has consistently helped me to uncomplicate my life,
to trust God and to do what he says.

Our relationship with God is meant to be enjoyed, not endured. My
relationship with God is the greatest joy in my life. It brings me much
laughter and sometimes tears, wonderful memories and great dreams
for the future. It is a relationship in which I can be myself and yet be fully
accepted, because I know that God loves me. He's my Dad, and I get to
be his daughter!

God and You

1. *How has your relationship with your physical father or a father figure shaped your attitudes and your concept of what our heavenly Father is like?*

2. *What must change in your understanding for you to view God as your perfect Father?*

3. *How do you respond to godly discipline? Do you accept that it is in your best interest? If not, how will you change?*

4. *While undergoing God's discipline, what scriptures would encourage and help you the most to have a proper perspective? Write them down and begin memorizing them, so that you will be prepared for the next time you undergo his discipline.*

25
Exact Representation
God, the Son

DENNIS YOUNG
Boston, USA

"For God so loved the world that he gave his one and only Son,
that whoever believes in him shall not perish but have eternal life."

John 3:16

If you had to choose someone to represent your family, who would
it be? What would they be like? Would you choose a lawyer who could
get to the point or a politician who could always put a good face on any
situation? Would it be a scholar to suggest education or a nurse to say,
"we care"?

Faced with this kind of situation, God made the decision that the
"divine family," the "us" of Genesis 1:26 would be represented on earth
by his son, Jesus. His entry into history was to be the pivotal event of all
time. The past had pointed to it and the future would look back on it. With
his coming, the world would never be the same. Men and women would
now face an eternal decision based on how God revealed, represented and
conveyed the love of the family from which Jesus had come.

Father and Son

There are two remarkable ways in which the Son reveals God: in the
relationship we see between the Father and the Son, and in the Son
himself. First, it is clear from the Scriptures that God wanted us to
understand him through this father/son relationship. More than 125
times in the New Testament, Jesus is referred to as or called the "Son of
God." Of all the ways God could have chosen to represent and reveal
himself to mankind—a cloud or a force or a mysterious being—he chose
to show us a son with a father, an intimate relationship. God wants us
to hear and see this relationship!

We hear the Father say in Matthew 17:5, "This is my Son, whom I love; with him I am well pleased. Listen to him!" In Hebrews 1, he lauds his Son as he describes angels worshiping him, the authority of his reign and his place at the Father's own right hand. In every book of the New Testament, God is a father who holds up his son and all that he has done, and a father who grieves over the end of his son's brief life.

Love flowed from Son to Father as well. We hear a son saying "my Father" again and again (over fifty times in the Gospels alone), a son who is proud to speak about his father. Hear the relationship. Jesus, a thirty-year-old man, saying "my Father" when the world would say, "Stand on your own two feet; be your own man." Hear Jesus' last words, "Father, into your hands I commit my spirit" (Luke 23:46).

These are the words of a son. They are not the words of a Lone Ranger type or someone who pulls himself up by his own bootstraps, a child prodigy or a self-made, self-actualized, self-educated religious guru. They are the words of a dependent, committed and faithful son. Do we understand that it should be "my Father" with us today no less than it was with Jesus then? Do we understand that God wants to have that same relationship with us?

Double Take

For God was pleased to have all his fullness dwell in [the Son], and through him to reconcile to himself all things. (Colossians 1:19-20)

The Son is the radiance of God's glory and the exact representation of his being. (Hebrews 1:3)

Second, God wants to be seen in the Son. The word "fullness" means "full measure, the entire contents." The word "representation" means "the exact expression." In Jesus we find the entire contents of who God is and the exact expression of the nature of God. Think about it. For a short span of years, this world saw in the Son the entire contents, the full measure and the perfect expression of God.

Trying hard to imagine this, I think about my four-year-old son, Dean, and how people often say to us, "He is a little Dennis!" I also think of my good friend Jaime who is in his thirties and is a devoted disciple, and I try to imagine God as a man his age. God wanted to live in this world as a young man. He would also die in this world as a young man. And as tragic and painful as his death was, the lasting impression and memory that God left with us is that of a young man. That is how his "entire contents," his "exact expression," could best be displayed. He wanted us to see his emotions, his love, his truth, his honesty, his commitment, his power, his humor, and his desire and drive to save all men.

Jesus is real, up close and personal. We see his righteous anger as a young man clearing out the temple. We see him grieve and weep next to the grave of his friend. We are moved by his compassion as we watch him help the sick. He shares with the poor. He loves the elderly. He extends the appeal of God, "Follow me." As a young man, he teaches us with authority, not in a condescending way, but in a challenging, humble, humorous, wise and encouraging way. His affection draws us in and makes us feel needed, wanted, welcome and part of his family. His patience and confidence as a young man are solid as he faces the proud, hypocritical, self-seeking, power hungry leaders of his day. His trust in his Father in the middle of the worst possible circumstances powerfully calls for us to imitate him. And lastly, the smile of the young son still reminds us that the God of the universe cares about the eternity of every single one of us. He has chosen his only Son to make this known.

The importance of this relationship has become more real to me in the last year. I have a number of friends who are dying of terminal illnesses. The reality of meeting their God becomes a more imminent possibility every day. As I accompany them through this challenging time, the sense of mystery and the fear of the unknown have been replaced more and more with the understanding that God is a Father and a Son. He has gone to great lengths to help us understand that his relationship with each of us is no different today. He has shown us that what awaits us eternally can be found in the Son in whom he chose to reveal himself to this world—the young Son, Jesus.

God and You

1. *How often do you refer to God as "my Father" in your relationship with him?*

2. *When was the last time you considered that God wanted you to understand him as a son or daughter with his father?*

3. *List the qualities of God that you see in his Son, Jesus.*

4. *Consider facing your own death now. What do you need to grow in to have the Father/son or Father/daughter relationship with God to make that transition confidently?*

26
Third Person
God, the Holy Spirit

BRIAN FELUSHKO
Toronto, Canada

If you are a disciple of Jesus, you have, no doubt, wondered what being with Jesus in the flesh would have been like. To see the expressions on his face, to hear the intonations of his voice, to touch his hand—we think it would help us so much if we could experience the physical presence of our Lord, even for a few moments. We read with longing what John writes:

> That which was from the beginning, which we have heard, which we have seen with our eyes, which we have looked at and our hands have touched—this we proclaim concerning the Word of life. (1 John 1:1)

Most of us do not realize that we have something better in our lives than the physical presence of the Son of God. Because of this, the disciples who actually walked with Jesus had no better opportunity to know God than we do today. In fact, it was for their good (and ours) that Jesus left them! Listen to the words of the Son of God:

> "Now I am going to him who sent me, yet none of you asks me, 'Where are you going?' Because I have said these things, you are filled with grief. But I tell you the truth: It is *for your good* that I am going away. Unless I go away, the Counselor will not come to you; but if I go, I will send him to you." (John 16:5-7, emphasis added)

What Jesus said to his disciples back then, he is saying to us today. When he left, he would not leave them or us as orphans. The Holy Spirit of God would come and live in their lives and in our lives. Their bodies and ours would become temples of the Holy Spirit (see 1 Corinthians 6:19). The doctrine of the Holy Spirit is the Biblical teaching that God is with us and in us. As Father, he provides for us. As Son, he lays down his life for us. As Spirit, he fills us, empowers us, encourages us and guides us. So significant is the Spirit's work in us that Jesus teaches in John 16 that it is better to have the Holy Spirit in us than to have the Son of God physically with us. Do you believe this? Why should you long to see, hear or touch the Son of God when you know you have the Spirit of God *in* you?

Transforming Presence

We are sinners and our sin separates us from God. We need that sin to be forgiven. But because we are sinners, we also need a new power greater than our own so that we can live the new life that God's forgiveness has made possible. It is only by the working of God's Spirit in our lives that we can possibly live faithful, fruitful lives for God. Our lives will not be transformed, nor will our world be evangelized, by human effort (Galatians 3:1-5).

We must learn what it means to be led by God's Spirit, for that is the only way we will be able to overcome the sinful nature:

> For if you live according to the sinful nature, you will die; but if by the Spirit you put to death the misdeeds of the body, you will live, because those who are led by the Spirit of God are sons of God. (Romans 8:13-14)

We must learn what it means to be filled with the Holy Spirit because that is where we will find the boldness to preach Jesus to a lost world (Acts 4:8-12, 4:23-31). We must learn how it is that we "grieve the Holy Spirit" (Ephesians 4:30) and "put out the Spirit's fire" (1 Thessalonians 5:19). Then we can turn away from those things that would limit or even inhibit his work in our lives. We must be a Spirit-led and a Spirit-filled people, bearing his fruit in our lives and being transformed into Jesus' likeness:

> But the fruit of the Spirit is love, joy, peace, patience, kindness, goodness, faithfulness, gentleness and self-control. Against such things there is no law. (Galatians 5:22-23)

> Now the Lord is the Spirit, and where the Spirit of the Lord is, there is freedom. And we, who with unveiled faces all reflect the Lord's

glory, are being transformed into his likeness with ever-increasing glory, which comes from the Lord, who is the Spirit. (2 Corinthians 3:17-18)

As the Spirit changes us, God convicts the world of sin, righteousness and the judgment to come (John 16:8-11). We need to understand in a much deeper way that God has sealed us with his Holy Spirit, a deposit guaranteeing what is coming (Ephesians 1:13-14); that God indeed "did not give us a spirit of timidity, but a spirit of power, love and self-discipline" (2 Timothy 1:7). We can live the life God has called us to because the Spirit who raised Jesus from the dead lives in us (Romans 8:9-11).

Spirit-Filled

Reading this chapter is not enough. We must dig into the Scriptures, as individuals and as a church. We must get to know God, the Holy Spirit, and all that he does for us—and wants to do in us and through us. Make a commitment to God that you are going to do whatever it takes to become a Spirit-led and Spirit-filled disciple of Christ. Pray that God will open up your mind and heart to the Holy Spirit as you study passages like John 14-16, Romans 8:1-27, 1 Corinthians 6:9-20 and Galatians 5:16-25. I would recommend to you Douglas Jacoby's book *The Spirit,** and encourage you to thoroughly study chapters one through fifteen. Humbly ask the evangelists and elders in your church to do some deeper teaching on the Holy Spirit in the disciple's life.

May the very Spirit that transformed the disciples from being fearful and self-preserving (John 20:19) into bold, courageous gospel proclaimers (Acts 4:18-20, 5:29-32) have his way also with us. Then the world in our generation will know that Jesus Christ is Lord, both by our lives and through our words.

---

*Douglas Jacoby, *The Spirit* (Woburn, Mass.: Discipleship Publications International, 1998).

God and You

1. *How does knowing that you have the gift of the Holy Spirit affect your daily life? Do you consciously reflect on that fact when you are making daily decisions?*

2. *What does it mean to you to be "led by the Spirit?" How would you know if the Holy Spirit were leading you?*

3. *What does it mean to you to be "filled with the Holy Spirit"? How can you know if you are filled with the Holy Spirit?*

4. *Whom do you know better; God the Father, God the Son or God the Holy Spirit? Why? Have you ever done a thorough study from the Scriptures about the Holy Spirit? Get some input and devise a plan for getting to know God's Spirit.*

GOD IS HERE

27
Always Here
Aware of God

RUSS EWELL
San Francisco, USA

Don't burn out; keep yourselves fueled and aflame. Be alert servants of the Master.

Romans 12:11, The Message

The person who comes to this chapter feeling like his or her life is in balance will find little here. This writing is for the harried, helpless and hapless. Here, the individual who is struggling to remain committed to God will find sustenance. The leader who is questioning whether or not he or she wants to continue carrying responsibility for the lives of others will find strength in this place. Those who have fallen into sin and don't feel like they can walk with confidence again will find new hope in these words.

We who hear the footsteps of failure close on our trail and who can't seem to escape the humbling impact of life's sins and mistakes have much to gain by increasing our awareness of God. We are the spiritually burnt out, those whose fervor is waning, and we must begin radical change today in order to avoid the destructive consequences of spiritual decay.

The first step in the process of renewal is to take an objective look at your life and to not be afraid to answer the following questions truthfully: Do you find yourself lacking the motivation to remain faithful to God? Are you growing more and more cynical about the kingdom of God? Do you see yourself withdrawing from relationships? Is there a disturbing trend of repeated sin in your life, especially during times of increased pressure? Can you spot uncontrollable anger, constant marital conflict or a decreased desire for intimacy in relationships? Are you suffering from chronic feelings of guilt and an unwillingness to discuss your problems? Do you see an increase in bitterness, and can you find its root in unfulfilled expectations? These are just a few symptoms which indicate that you have lost your spiritual fervor (Romans 12:11, NIV) or have reached a point of spiritual burnout (Romans 12:11, The Message). The steps below will get you on your way toward recovery and repentance, and before long you will see your passion for God and life return.

Heightened Awareness

We must be aware of God's love. In the church, there is too little talk of God's love and altogether too little awareness of this powerful aspect of his person and character. We must look at all the answered prayers, forgiven sins and tender handling from God so that we can see and appreciate his love. An awareness of God begins with understanding that God desires a relationship of the most intimate kind with each one of us. David declares that God's love is better than life itself (Psalm 63:3). If we want to get up from sin, failure and frustration, then we have to reorient our value system so that we are ecstatic over the simple yet elegant truth that God treasures us. Next to that, no human audience can compare.

We must also be aware of his absence. Jeremiah warns of the curse that comes with relying on the flesh when he speaks of being a "bush in the wastelands" and dwelling "in the parched places of the desert" (Jeremiah 17:5-6). While many of us give lip service to the curse of neglecting our relationship with God, very rarely do we identify the consequences of this neglect: spiritual loneliness. We must allow ourselves to be sobered by this grim warning and turn our hearts toward God (Jeremiah 17:7-8).

An awareness of God's timing is necessary as well. Two of the greatest sources of stress in our lives are change and unfulfilled expectations. Translation? When we realize that we do not have control over the timing in our lives, we can panic or become frustrated. David again provides the calming solution: he puts his trust in God, knowing that "[his] times are in God's hands" (Psalm 31:14-15). We reduce the anxious striving of life when we trust that God is in control and wants to make our dreams come true.

Additionally, we must develop an awareness of God's protection. Proverbs 3:25 encourages us to have no fear of sudden disaster. We can all have a sense of potential disaster when working on a project at work or when our children are away from us or when we are about to confess sin. We fear that somehow we will end up exposed and vulnerable to the danger of destructive human action. When we are aware of God's protection (Psalm 5:11, Psalm 34:5), then we will soar with confidence again, regardless of the circumstances we are facing.

A further crucial conviction is an awareness of God's forgiveness. One of the most distressing and discouraging experiences we can have as disciples is to be under the burdening strain of constant guilt. The simplest cure for this is to be open about the sin in our lives. But even when we have properly dealt with our sin, greater complications can arise if we lack the faith to believe God has truly forgiven us. I would wager that for every person held up by the guilt of unconfessed sin, there are two held up by the guilt of an accused conscience that will not let go of past sin. We must cling to God's willingness to forgive, clearly portrayed by Jeremiah's depiction of God as a potter willing to take the marred clay and reshape it rather than discard it (Jeremiah 18:4).

We must also learn to be aware of God's power. Many of us don't believe that a Christian can burn out. Yet the Bible refers to the curse of not relying on God, which could certainly mean that, disconnected from the power of God, man will burn out in this life. Proverbs 24:10 amplifies this thought as it describes the inadequate strength of men who fail under pressure. I believe that the man being referred to is one who has lost awareness of God's power in his life and who is attempting to do everything through his own strength. His only hope of renewal is to rely on God's strength for the tasks that lie before him.

Finally, we must develop an abiding awareness of God in our hearts. Ephesians 4:18 describes a person with a hard heart as one who ignores God. We can infer that this hardening happens when we ignore our sin. If sin is not acknowledged, the heart becomes comfortable with its constant presence and less sensitive to the presence of God. The moment by moment awareness of God becomes obscured. Only the pursuit of a pure heart will allow us to see God at work in our lives (Matthew 5:8, Psalm 10:4).

Refocusing

The three Ds of burnout—discouragement, despair and distress—have more to do with losing focus on God than almost anything else. When they consume our lives, there is no room for God. When we are consumed with God's presence in our lives (Psalm 114:7), there is no room for them.

God and You

1. With how many of the symptoms in the third paragraph could you identify?

2. Do you believe you are a person who values awareness of God? How do you know?

3. What are your personal warning signs that you are approaching spiritual burnout?

4. What can you do today to put God at the center of your life and thoughts?

28
Stand Amazed
In Awe of God

Dave Eastman
Los Angeles, USA

> Lord, I have heard of your fame;
> I stand in awe of your deeds, O Lord.
>
> Habakkuk 3:2

Standing in awe of God: In a world without Satan, this would be as natural as waking up or breathing. Why? Because God is awesome! He is phenomenal. His power is incomparable. He has no peer. As Ethan the Ezrahite wrote:

> In the council of the holy ones God is greatly feared;
> he is more awesome than all who surround him. (Psalm 89:7)

But how do we, in our finite, limited understanding, comprehend a God who is by definition infinite and limitless? It is my conviction that until we are free of the shackles of our imperfect, sinful minds and bodies, we will never completely understand our God. However, even in this life we must not shrink back from striving to know him much more deeply than we do. Let us consider together the God whom we love and serve that we may stand in awe of his greatness.

The Creative Power of God

> Who has measured the waters in the hollow of his hand,
> or with the breadth of his hand marked off the heavens?
> (Isaiah 40:12)

The oceans to which Isaiah refers cover over seventy percent of the earth's surface and comprise somewhere in the neighborhood of 370 quadrillion gallons. And yet God didn't use a giant tank or even a big bucket to measure them out—he did it in the hollow of his hand! If you were to move a handful of water, roughly one ounce at a time, into an empty trench every minute, it would take about ninety trillion years to create the oceans. If the whole world got involved in ocean creating, six billion hands could do the job in a short 15,000 years. Are you in awe of God?

Next we are told that God marked off the heavens with the "breadth of his hand," the distance between the end of the pinky and the end of the thumb when fully extended. Now get this: A beam of light—which can circle the entire earth seven times in one second—takes approximately 750,000 years just to get to our nearest neighboring galaxy of Andromeda. There are millions of galaxies that fill our universe. Yet God measured it all off with the breadth of his hand. He is awesome in his creative power!

The Sustaining Power of God

God not only conceived and fashioned the universe, but he also sustains it—moment by moment and day by day. God waters every plant, sustains every animal and provides sunshine, rain and nutrients in the soil. In short, he takes care of his creation.

But it is not about the botanical and animal world that God is most concerned. He is deeply concerned with our needs. He gives to us physically, spiritually, emotionally and intellectually. When we open ourselves up to the influence of his perfect word, he protects our minds and redeems our hearts. He cares about our next meal and our next day. He knows every hair on every head. (Some of us are making it easier for him as the number of hairs on our heads is rapidly decreasing!) He puts people in our lives to bring us to Christ, to rebuke us when we are in sin, to encourage us daily and to train and disciple us. He gives us just what we need when we need it. God is awesome in his sustaining power.

The Intellectual Power of God

If the physical power of God is not daunting enough for us, let us consider the power of his mind. Everything in God's creation is a product of the creative genius of the Almighty. The order of the universe, the angle of earth to sun, the atmosphere of the earth, the magnetic fields, the process of photosynthesis, the food chain, the human eye, the design of every atom, molecule, microorganism, plant, insect, animal and human—all attest to a God with an infinitely superior intellect. He envisions a thing—works it out in his mind—and then simply speaks it into existence.

It may help us to consider our own limitations. At the time of this writing, I am discipling eight men, and my wife is discipling eight women. My sector consists of 264 disciples. I am hard pressed to deeply consider on a daily basis the ongoing needs of eight men. I try to pray for every soul in my sector at least once weekly, and it stretches me. And yet:

> From heaven the Lord looks down
> and sees all mankind;
> from his dwelling place he watches
> all who live on earth—
> he who forms the hearts of all,
> who considers everything they do. (Psalm 33:13-15)

While I fumble around mentally with my little group of eight, God considers the motives, the thoughts, the actions and the future of six billion people simultaneously. He knows every thought in every heart on every street in every neighborhood in every town and city of every nation on every continent on the globe. He records the sins of the unsaved, sorts through the multitudes looking for those whose hearts are open, arranges meetings, dispatches angels and answers millions of prayers daily—all the while taking care of his creation, holding every-thing together and dealing forcefully with Satan and his demonic hordes. And somehow, in his infinite holiness and capacity, he loves each one of us much more than we love our own children!

One day Philip the evangelist was in a city in Samaria. God knew of an Ethiopian in a chariot riding on the road from Jerusalem to Gaza. Sychar, a representative city in Samaria, is about twenty-eight miles from Jerusalem and sixty-five or so from Gaza. The Ethiopian was reading Isaiah 53. God knew that he would not understand it, so he dispatched Philip from Samaria, on foot, to intercept the Ethiopian. God had to work out all the timing so that Philip, after walking maybe thirty to forty miles, would intercept the official a certain number of miles from a small body of water on that road. Philip initiated a conversation with the man and got into his chariot. Shortly after explaining the plan of salvation, they reached this oasis in the desert so that the man could get baptized (Acts 8:26-40). Are you impressed with God yet?

Our generation is shallow, fickle, demanding and easily bored. We would rather watch a film than read; enjoy a game than think; and be spoon fed insights instead of spending the hours in deep thought and meditation that lead us to conviction and awe. We must ensure that this is not true of us as disciples. We, of all people on the globe, enjoying the privileges of salvation and the hope of heaven, must take the time to think, to pray, to meditate on our God until we all, like the great prophet Ezekiel, are knocked off our feet, overwhelmed at the greatness and majesty of our awesome God (Ezekiel 1:28).

God and You

1. *Do you consider yourself a deep, thoughtful and meditative person? If not, how can you become one?*

2. *Read Job 37:22-42:6. In view of the greatness of God, is your response similar to that of Job?*

3. *How much time do you typically spend in praising God before you take your list of needs to him? This week, spend the first five to ten minutes of each prayer time in praise and meditation.*

4. *Read Isaiah 6:1-5. Compare your own view of God, and your ensuing reaction, with that of Isaiah.*

29

Easy Access
Near to God

SAM POWELL
New York City, USA

> How great is the love the Father has lavished on us, that we should be called children of God! And that is what we are!

> 1 John 3:1

How amazing indeed is God's love for us! There should be no question as to God's desire to have a special relationship with us. We are the most treasured of all his creation, and he has spared nothing for our redemption and salvation. The cross alone proclaims his incomparable love for undeserving sinners. How intense is our desire to be close to the Lord God? To have the relationship with God that he longs for and that we so desperately need, we must pray to have a lasting change of heart.

Desire to Know Him

Puerto Rican heartthrob Ricky Martin showed up in Manhattan for an autograph session for his latest CD and was met by more than eight thousand screaming, fanatical teenagers. The youths lined up as early as 5:00 AM for a 4:00 PM signing at Tower Records. Streets had to be closed and security increased because of these zealots who would stop at nothing for a glimpse of their superstar. They love Ricky, they dream of Ricky, they worship Ricky and they have eyes only for Ricky.

Sadly, the fervor of these teens for their pop star often puts to shame the passion that God's children have for him. The Lord God is so much more deserving of our love and praise. To draw near to him, as we need to, we must rekindle the fires of appreciation and thankfulness. We must desire with all our hearts to love him, know him and walk with him.

O God, you are my God,
    earnestly I seek you;
my soul thirsts for you,
    my body longs for you,
in a dry and weary land
    where there is no water....
Because your love is better than life,
    my lips will glorify you.
I will praise you as long as I live,
    and in your name I will lift up my hands.
My soul will be satisfied as with the richest of foods;
    with singing lips my mouth will praise you. (Psalm 63:1-8)

The desire to be with God that David expresses should be in the heart of every soul who has been redeemed by the blood of the Lamb. The love God has for us needs to create a burning desire in our souls to want to draw near him. Where would we be if not for his mercy and grace? We must stop, be still, meditate and allow our callous and forgetful hearts to be pricked by the incredible goodness of a long-suffering God. No longer should we disappoint him with neglect and aloofness. He is waiting. Where are we?

"How often I have longed to gather your children together, as a hen gathers her chicks under her wings, but you were not willing." (Matthew 23:37)

Declare His Praises

After over a decade of being single in the kingdom of God, a dear sister and friend has found the right man. Not known to be one who shows much emotion, she is now giddy and excited and cannot stop talking about her knight in shining armor. Without hesitation she tells all who will listen that he is handsome, intelligent and spiritual—and the list goes on. In her mind he is worthy of such praise.

In a much greater way, we need to sing God's praises daily:

But you are a chosen people, a royal priesthood, a holy nation, a people belonging to God, that you may declare the praises of him who called you out of darkness into his wonderful light. (1 Peter 2:9)

Our hearts need to focus on the goodness and the greatness of God. He has called us out of darkness to declare to the world how awesome he is. We must remind ourselves of his magnificence, not because he *needs* our praise, but because our hearts need to be humbled by his greatness. We stop drawing near to God when we forget who he is and all that he has done for us. This has always been a problem for God's people. The time has come to no longer take for granted what we have in Christ!

The list of attributes for which God can be praised is endless. We must make time to say aloud how majestic and glorious our creator is, for he is worthy of such praise:

Many, O Lord my God,
    are the wonders you have done.
The things you planned for us
    no one can recount to you;
were I to speak and tell of them,
    they would be too many to declare. (Psalm 40:5)

Decide to Change

I recently met up with a fellow member of my sports club whom I had not seen in weeks and was impressed by the amount of weight he had lost. I asked him how he did it. He said he woke up one morning and simply decided that enough was enough—no gimmicks or fads, just a decision to be radically consistent. Daily exercise and a reasonable diet led to his victory over body fat.

Jesus understood the need for daily decisions about his time with God. No one was closer to the Father than Jesus. His life teaches us that we must deny our flesh and decide to seek God first:

Very early in the morning, while it was still dark, Jesus got up, left the house and went off to a solitary place, where he prayed. (Mark 1:35)

But Jesus often withdrew to lonely places and prayed. (Luke 5:16)

Jesus refused to allow fatigue or other obstacles to keep him from having time with the One from whom he received his strength. Being near to God is more than a quiet time; it is all about how you live and your understanding of God's presence in your life. However, this does not negate our need to set aside time for God alone. The Lord is with you when you are with him. If you seek him, he will be found by you, but if you forsake him, he will forsake you (2 Chronicles 15:2).

Let's not fool ourselves. At times we are excuse makers, and we love the easy path. But there is a price to be paid for being close to God: the intense effort it takes to focus on him. It is a daily decision, one which demands that we become habitually radical. Like my friend at the gym, we will change only when we get disgusted with what we see in ourselves and conclude that enough is enough. *I will no longer be sloppy and undisciplined in my relationship with God.* Decide! Decide! Decide today and every day that you will give your heart, soul and mind to the Lord God.

> "I will bring him near and he will come close to me,
>   for who is he who will devote himself to be close
> to me?"   '
>   declares the Lord. (Jeremiah 30:21)

God and You

1. *How deep is your desire to grow in your knowledge and appreciation of the Lord?*

2. *How often do you focus on just praising and exalting God?*

3. *Are you willing to be radical to make time to be with God?*

4. *How does it affect your heart to know how much God longs to be close to you?*

30

Just Like Him
Imitating God

BARBARA PORTER
Sao Paulo, Brazil

Imitate God? It's already pretty overwhelming to try to imitate Jesus—imagine imitating God! At least Jesus shared in our humanity. I have heard my whole life that we are made in God's image, but we often seem so very far from that. I know the Bible teaches we should imitate God, but is this really attainable?

Help from Above

In many ways, truly imitating God is impossible. We will never be sovereign, omniscient, omnipotent creators. Nevertheless, we are commanded: "Be perfect, therefore, as your heavenly Father is perfect" (Matthew 5:48). If God asks us to imitate him, we must believe that it is possible to obey and that God himself will enable us to do so.

Romans 8:29 reveals one of God's deepest desires for our lives: "For those God foreknew he also predestined to be conformed to the likeness of his Son." Ephesians 4:22-24 goes on to say that we have been taught to put off our old, sinful selves, and to put on the new self, created to be like God in true righteousness and holiness.

And Colossians 3:9-10 describes the goal of our lives, now that we have taken off our old self with its practices and have put on the new self, which is being renewed in knowledge in the image of its Creator. This new self, acquired when disciples repent (put off the old self) and are baptized, is created to become like God.

God's eternal purpose is to transform us into his children, resembling him in his very nature. We are not merely supposed to do "religious things," though they may be doctrinally correct; God wants us to be like him in our hearts and in our attitudes. These verses reveal that imitating God is not only possible, but is—and has been since the beginning of creation—God's will for all true Christians. How inspiring and encouraging this is: God himself is actively involved in helping us to reach this challenging spiritual goal!

Dearly Loved Children

The Bible teaches us not only that we should imitate God, but also how and why:

> Be imitators of God, therefore, as dearly loved children and live a life of love, just as Christ loved us and gave himself up for us as a fragrant offering and sacrifice to God. (Ephesians 5:1-2)

First of all, we see the strong connection between imitating God and being dearly loved children. Who are, by nature, the best imitators? Children! Children imitate naturally, without being encouraged, exhorted or taught. It amazes me how many of my mannerisms and facial expressions I see in my six-year-old daughter, Jacqueline. When she talks, she uses her hands and opens her eyes really wide—I feel like I'm looking in the mirror! Jacqueline is quite a strong-willed little girl with definite opinions and preferences. Yet, although she tries very hard to be her own, independent self, she cannot help but imitate.

As Christians, we are not just any children; we are "dearly loved" children. This makes a big difference! From time to time we hear about children with neglectful, abusive parents. Sadly, such children frequently end up imitating these very negative qualities by default. Others are so revolted by the bad example of their parents that they want nothing to do with their lifestyle. By contrast, dearly loved children want to be like their parents. If we understand how much we are loved by God, we will eagerly desire to imitate all of his wonderful qualities.

Servants Like Him

What is it about God that we should imitate? Where do we start? Philippians 2:5-8 gives us incredible insight into this question:

> Your attitude should be the same as that of Christ Jesus:
>
>> Who, being in very nature God,
>>   did not consider equality with God something
>>   to be grasped,
>> but made himself nothing,

> taking the very nature of a servant,
> being made in human likeness.
> And being found in appearance as a man,
> he humbled himself
> and became obedient to death—
> even death on a cross!

Jesus was in very nature God. Yet, unbelievably, he did not demand the exalted status due him. How then are we to imitate God? By making ourselves nothing, serving those around us, giving ourselves up for others and living a life of love. Think honestly about your life. Do you live a life of love or a life of legalistic commitment? Is your sacrifice to God your duty or a "fragrant offering" lifted up to him?

It has been a tremendous privilege to return to Brazil and to lead the women in the Sao Paulo church. The disciples here are very grateful and have giving, sacrificial hearts. One sister's story moved my heart in a special way. Givonete, a mother of four children, persevered for two years before seeing her husband, William, baptized into Christ. A short time later, the family began to have serious financial problems, aggravated when William lost his job. He remained firm in his faith amidst these challenges and shared his faith with Luiza, a forty-year-old single mother. Luiza, full of joy and immense gratitude, was baptized.

Some time later, Givonete and William began to weaken in their faith and to struggle spiritually. Luiza was so thankful for her salvation that she invited William's family of six to stay in the rear part of her very simple house, rent free. She gladly provided the family with food and helped them get back on their feet. William and Givonete were so touched by the love and generosity of Luiza that they regained their spiritual strength and found the faith to recover financially.

God recently blessed Luiza's sacrificial heart with an entire busload of personal visitors at a "Bring Your Neighbor Day" worship service. Luiza is a woman who gives up her life for others. For whom are you giving up your life? Do you live a life of religious activity or a life of love? Are you a church member or an imitator of God?

Spiritually Responsible

Whose responsibility is it for us to imitate God? *We* have the responsibility to get rid of our sinful practices, and the *Holy Spirit* renews us in the image of God. That is, as we decide—and it takes a firm decision—to continually repent and to try to imitate God, the Spirit can transform us "into [God's] likeness with ever-increasing glory" (2 Corinthians 3:18). The more we strive to know and love God, to understand and appreciate his tremendous love for us, the more we will yearn to imitate him. What a responsibility! What a privilege! What an opportunity!

God and You

1. *What is the difference between doing religious things and imitating God?*

2. *Who is someone for whom you are giving up your life? How are you "making yourself nothing" for this person?*

3. *What hinders you from imitating God?*

4. *In what specific ways can you change in order to live a life of love?*

31

Heart's Delight

Enjoying God

THOMAS JONES
Boston, USA

Delight yourself in the Lord
and he will give you the desires of your heart.

Psalm 37:4

David's statement here in Psalm 37 literally means it is God's will for us to take great pleasure in him. It is not his plan that we just obey him and trudge along the road of faith, grimly trying to hold on until the end. We need to fear, honor, obey, serve and glorify God—and at the same time, *enjoy him*. He wants us to get joy from him and from our walk with him. He wants to delight us. There is an old Protestant creed that says the chief duty of man is to glorify God and enjoy him forever. The creed was off the mark on a number of points, but I am coming to realize that it got that part right—God is most pleased when we find our highest pleasure in him.

Decision Needed

David's words in Psalm 37:4 are in the form of an admonition or command. This would seem to indicate that enjoying God isn't always the natural thing to do, even by those who know him quite well. Behind some of the faces you see at church are people who are going about the business of being disciples, but are not enjoying God. There are times when we just need to be told: "Look at life differently. Delight yourself in the Lord. Just enjoy him and what he is doing."

Someone may say, "But if you have to *tell* a person to enjoy something, isn't there something wrong with the picture?" Not really. At different times in my life, I have had friends tell me "Tom, what you need to do is go home and enjoy your family" or "What you need to do is take your wife to dinner and just enjoy her." These were always helpful challenges that brought good results.

We need to ask ourselves from time to time, "Am I enjoying God?" If we are not, we don't have to wait for some feeling to mysteriously wash over us or for the church to plan some special program. We can immediately remind ourselves that our God *is* an awesome God, and we can decide that we are going to delight in him.

Enjoying God's Grace

When you enjoy another person and your relationship with them, it is usually because of certain qualities they have. Maybe they are funny or inspiring or full of wisdom. Maybe they are always making you better. Enjoying the God described in this book means enjoying his qualities and enjoying what he is doing in our lives. Let me give two examples. You can add many more.

Start by enjoying God's grace. Paul describes God as one who "richly provides us with everything for our enjoyment" (1 Timothy 6:17). His point is that whatever God gives, he gives for us to enjoy. In context, Paul says that God gave us food for that purpose, and also marriage. But if everything God gives is for our enjoyment, then certainly his greatest gift—the grace that comes in Christ—is meant to be enjoyed.

Paul tells us in Ephesians 1:8 that God has "lavished" his grace on us. The *American Heritage Dictionary* defines "lavish" as

1. Characterized by or produced with extravagance and profusion.
2. Immoderate in giving or bestowing; unstinting. To give or bestow in abundance.

God didn't just give grace. He gave it in abundance; he gave it immoderately.

Why was he so extravagant with grace? First, I suspect it was because we all need a lot of it! But also, because he wanted us to have a lot of it to enjoy. Don't get nervous here. I am not talking about using grace as an excuse for sin. But I am saying we need to enjoy our forgiveness, enjoy our freedom in Christ, enjoy the fact that our relationship with God is not based on our performance and enjoy that our destiny is in heaven.

I recall times when our children were younger when my wife and I would give one of them a gift. If we later came in and saw her just having a blast with it, we didn't say, "Now, young lady, we gave this to you because we wanted you to have it and we wanted you to feel loved, but we really don't want you enjoying the gift this much." No, if we found her having a great time with it—and using it in the right way! — we were thrilled. Surely God is thrilled when we enjoy his grace and then let it motivate us to live more godly lives. If you have never been told to enjoy grace, let me tell you now.

Enjoying God's Surprises

Most of us enjoy movies with surprises and plot twists. The drama that God is playing out in the world is full of these. God loves to turn the tables. God loves to overthrow humanistic thinking and stand it on its ear. God loves to take weakness and show his power in it.

> But God chose the foolish things of the world to shame the wise; God chose the weak things of the world to shame the strong. He chose the lowly things of this world and the despised things—and the things that are not—to nullify the things that are. (1 Corinthians 1:27-28)

When God does this, can't you just imagine him smiling? Nobody thought the foolish or the weak or the despised things could be used for good. The enemy certainly didn't. He thought he had things going his way, but God turned the tables on normal thinking.

Sports fans love to watch a team win who is not supposed to (unless their favorite team is beaten!). It is fun watching people beat the odds. We need to enjoy watching God work his surprises.

God is able to do anything he wants to do, but chooses to take the unlikely and then do the seemingly impossible. He took a nation of slaves and made them his chosen people. He took a stable and made it the birthplace of a savior. He took a despised cross and used it to show his extravagant grace. He took common and unlearned men and used them to light a fire that lit up a world. He took college-age dreamers in the 1970s and used them to take the gospel around the world in this generation. And he has more surprises in store. We need to sit back at times and just enjoy our surprising God.

More of a Good Thing

David says that when you delight yourself in the Lord, you will receive the desires of your heart. Some of us think that if we delight in the Lord, we will get the husband we want or a coveted job or a certain position in the kingdom. Let me offer another possibility: When we really start enjoying God and he becomes our highest joy, he is delighted to give us even more—of himself! May our awesome God help us to enjoy *him* forever!

God and You

1. *What do you think about the idea of enjoying God? Are you the kind of person that needs a reminder to enjoy God?*

2. *Do you err on the side of taking grace for granted, or do you need to learn to enjoy God's grace more? How can you get closer to balancing the two?*

3. *What other example could you give of how you need to enjoy God and the things that come from our relationship with him?*

4. *Is anyone you know going through the motions of the Christian life but not enjoying God? Be the person to gently help them to find joy in their walk with God.*

Epilogue

As this book goes to print, we have just celebrated the twentieth anniversary of the Boston Church of Christ. Thousands of disciples and friends gathered at the Fleet Center from all over the Boston area, grateful for what God has done in these past two decades. The church service centered around an incredible presentation of choral music and dramatic readings highlighting God's loving plan of redemption through the ages—from the creation to Pentecost. It was a deeply moving reminder that only God's grace and sovereignty are responsible for all that has happened in the church and in our lives. The service closed with dozens of baptisms, an indicator that what God has done so far is only the start!

A highlight of the day for me was watching a special edition of the Kingdom News Network (KNN), the video news magazine of the International Churches of Christ, focused on the events of these first twenty years. Beginning with a simple but radical plan, God has taken a small group of disciples in Boston and raised up a worldwide movement of 358 churches in 155 nations with over 200,000 in attendance. I was brought to tears to see how God has used ordinary men and women to accomplish such extraordinary things, and I remembered the words of Jesus:

> "Blessed are the eyes that see what you see. For I tell you that many prophets and kings wanted to see what you see but did not see it, and to hear what you hear but did not hear it." (Luke 10:23-24)

The video closed with a sober reminder that the "easiest" part of world evangelism has been done; we must rely on God as never before to see the dream of an evangelized world come true in this generation.

✧

Whenever we speak of "God's modern-day movement," we must always remember that the key word is "God." Our hope and desire is that this book has served to remind us about and inspire us with the greatness of the God we serve. No group can claim to be the movement of God without each individual striving to make his or her own life a movement of God. To understand him more intimately, more confidently, more clearly, must be a burning desire in the heart of every disciple.

Having served as a missionary in Paris, France, and Montreal, Canada, I spent a lot of time convincing people how worthwhile it is to know and love the God of the Bible. A phrase I often heard in Quebec was "God yes; religion no!" The world is searching for a true spiritual understanding of God—without all the religious hardware. Too many churches and religious institutions fit the description of what Paul saw in Athens:

"For as I walked around and looked carefully at your objects of worship, I even found an altar with this inscription: TO AN UNKNOWN GOD." (Acts 17:23a)

We can either bemoan the spiritual situation of our day, or boldly say like Paul,

"Now what you worship as something unknown I am going to proclaim to you." (Acts 17:23b)

Never has the call to know God been more pressing than it is today. The dream of world evangelism can only be accomplished by men and women who can confidently show God to the world. The torch of hope can be carried only by people striving to know him with all their hearts.

✧

Knowing God is what our lives are all about. Every disciple has received the encouraging call to love, trust, revere, obey, and find peace and joy in God. As we grow in his love and service, he will continue to lead us "in triumphal procession" (2 Corinthians 2:14). Let us daily fall down in worship and praise of his greatness. For truly, our God is an awesome God!

DEDE PETRE
Boston, USA
July 1999

Who Are We?

Discipleship Publications International (DPI) began publishing in 1993. We are a nonprofit Christian publisher affiliated with the International Churches of Christ, committed to publishing and distributing materials that honor God, lift up Jesus Christ and show how his message practically applies to all areas of life. We have a deep conviction that no one changes life like Jesus and that the implementation of his teaching will revolutionize any life, any marriage, any family and any singles household.

Since our beginning we have published more than 75 titles; plus we have produced a number of important, spiritual audio products. More than one million volumes have been printed, and our works have been translated into more than a dozen languages—international is not just a part of our name! Our books are shipped regularly to every inhabited continent.

To see a more detailed description of our works, find us on the World Wide Web at www.dpibooks.com. You can order books by calling 1-888-DPI-BOOK twenty-four hours a day. From outside the US, call 781-937-3883, ext. 231 during Boston-area business hours.

We appreciate the hundreds of comments we have received from readers. We would love to hear from you. Here are other ways to get in touch:

Mail: DPI, One Merrill St., Woburn, MA 01801
E-mail: dpibooks@icoc.org

Find us on the
World Wide Web

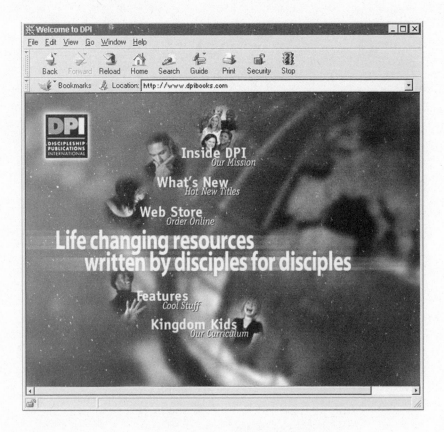

www.dpibooks.com
1-888-DPI-BOOK
outside US: 781-937-3883 x231